GEORGE III

Tyrant or Constitutional Monarch?

PROBLEMS IN EUROPEAN CIVILIZATION

UNDER THE EDITORIAL DIRECTION OF

Ralph W. Greenlaw* and Dwight E. Lee†

Other volumes in preparation

GEORGE III

Tyrant or Constitutional Monarch?

EDITED WITH AN INTRODUCTION BY

E. A. Reitan

ILLINOIS STATE UNIVERSITY

D. C. HEATH AND COMPANY · BOSTON

Englewood · Chicago · Dallas · San Francisco · Atlanta · London · Toronto

Table of Contents

Introduction

ERBERT Butterfield has written: "The most important, perhaps, of all the issues presented to us, and all the topics of controversy ever provoked, by the reign of George III, is the question of the framework of ideas and purposes which shaped the attitude and conditioned the conduct of that King at the beginning of the reign." [1] The problem is not simply one of unravelling the psychology of a very complex person. It is the familiar problem of determining, in an age of change, who is the radical and who is the conservative. The opponents of George III charged him with trying to alter the character of English government by increasing the power of the crown, and attributed to him the political turbulence of the first two decades of his reign. George III and his supporters insisted that he was struggling to preserve the rightful powers of the crown against the efforts of ambitious men to deprive it of its just powers and independence. This problem is still the central one in historical scholarship on the reign of George III.

The major facts are not in dispute. It is well known that George III had been raised in an environment of hostility toward George II and his ministers. The accession of George III to the throne in 1760 was accompanied by a shower of pamphlets and pronouncements which proclaimed intentions of political change. Contemporaries observed not only that new faces were present at court, but that a new spirit was evident. Within eighteen months the ministers of George II (Pitt and Newcastle) had left office, to be re-

[1] Herbert Butterfield, *George III and the Historians* (London, 1957), p. 216.

placed by the king's tutor and confidant, the Earl of Bute. In the full tide of victory the Duke of Bedford was sent to Paris with a splendid embassy to bring to a close the great war which Pitt and Newcastle had waged with such startling success. The peace treaty provoked a bitter debate, and after it had been approved Bute, weary of the burdens of office, insisted upon resigning. A series of weak, unstable ministries followed until the establishment of the ministry of Lord North in 1770. Out of this decade grew a constitutional controversy which was intensified by the War of American Independence and which reached its climax in the resignation of Lord North in 1782. The nature and origins of this controversy remain, to the present time, the center of a debate among historians which goes to the roots of eighteenth century government and politics. The selections in this volume have been chosen to illustrate and define the character of this debate and to bring into focus the status of current scholarship on the question.

Historical controversy concerning the intentions and actions of George III in the early part of his reign centers on four points. These are: 1) the objectives of George III at the beginning of his reign, 2) the personal ability of George III, 3) the relation of George III and his ministers and 4) the nature and role of political parties in the political developments of the time. Historians have held differing interpretations on each of these points. Directly or indirectly, the selections in this volume touch upon each of these four aspects of the problem, and in reading each selection the student should be alert to views expressed by the author on each of these four points.

I. CONTEMPORARY VIEWS

Favorable and unfavorable interpretations of George III developed during the course of his reign, and these have supplied the elements of the two main currents of interpretation since that time. The works of Nathanial Wraxall and John Adolphus illustrate the favorable or "Tory" interpretation of George III. In their respect for the institution of monarchy and their admiration for the public and private virtues of George III both of these writers demonstrate attitudes which were dominant in the latter part of the reign, when the king had become a revered symbol of national resistance to French ideas and French power.

Nathanial Wraxall was a traveller and professional man of letters who sat in parliament from 1780–1794, usually supporting the court. He emphasizes the personal virtues and good intentions of George III, without denying his political mistakes. He attributes some of George III's shortcomings to the isolation of his early life and the deficiencies of his education, but at no point does he accuse the king of arbitrary notions or an excessive love of power. He is unaware of the existence of an important constitutional issue, taking it for granted that George III was acting in accordance with the accepted role of a monarch. Wraxall's memoirs were first published in 1815, when the aged king was stricken by physical and mental illness. He wrote of a time when the king was at the height of his powers, recalling men who were already becoming dim in the public memory and recounting controversies over which the passage of time was casting a softening veil. Wraxall's portrayal of George III lies in the twilight zone where views based on personal knowledge and participation are passing, to be replaced by formal history.

A similar attitude toward George III is found in John Adolphus' *The History of England from the Accession to the Decease of King George the Third*. Adolphus states that George III planned to introduce important changes in the exercise of the royal power when his reign began, and he approves of the efforts of the king and Bute to free themselves from domination by the ministers of George II (Pitt and Newcastle). He defends the methods which they adopted as "a moderate exertion of the constitutional prerogative." He attributes the failure of this undertaking to the incapacity of Bute, and he blames the "insidious and baleful endeavours" of the opposition for the political turmoil of the first decade of the reign. Thus, Adolphus concludes, the well-intentioned efforts of George III to exercise the royal power brought political difficulties with them; "although he was enabled to break the established phalanx . . . the struggle was attended with many painful circumstances."

The "Tory" interpretation of Wraxall and Adolphus found a rival in the works of Edmund Burke and Horace Walpole. Burke and Walpole derived their views of the king from the bitter partisan strife of the first two decades of the reign, and they expressed in their works the views of the opposition to George III.

Edmund Burke's *Thoughts on the Causes of the Present Discontents* (1770) expounds the views of the opposition group led by the Marquis of Rockingham. Burke takes the position that from the beginning of the reign a deliberate and consistent effort had been made to increase the power of the crown, and he describes the insidious and complex methods which had been used to remove obstacles to royal power. He does not blame George III personally, but he adopts the familiar fiction of "the king's evil advisers," placing responsibility on a cabal of ambitious courtiers who did not hold responsible office but who pulled strings behind the scenes. These men made their actions seem plausible and public-spirited by stating high ideals, but the effect was to give rise to a system "which without directly violating any letter of any law, operates against the spirit of the whole constitution."

Under George I and George II, Burke argues, it was necessary for the crown to obtain the support of men of rank and property (such as Newcastle) or great personal popularity (such as Pitt). Thus the interests of monarchy were harmonized with those of the nation. With the accession of George III, however, an attempt was made to cast off this dependence and to rule through the influence of the crown alone. The method used, as Burke describes it, was an elaborate and cunning one. The first step of the cabal was to "destroy everything of strength which did not derive its principal nourishment from the court." Since Pitt derived his power from popularity, and Newcastle drew his from the "natural and fixed influence" of property and political connection, both of those men had to be overthrown. Having disposed of their rivals the courtiers then proceeded to introduce a system which would make certain that no new leaders could arise who might threaten the independent power of the crown. The first step was to set up as principal minister a man (Bute) who owed his power entirely to the court. When this move did not succeed they turned to a system by which ministers would ostensibly govern the country with the important decisions being made backstage. There was a constant shuffling of ministries, with dissension fomented among the ministers to prevent them from developing independence through solidarity. The members of the cabal exercised their power through secondary offices while "the first and most respectable persons in the kingdom are tossed about like tennis balls." This alteration in the relation of the king and his ministers was accompanied by an attempt to change the party system. Independent political parties were to be broken up and power centered in a party of "king's friends" whose loyalty was to the crown. The effect was to destroy the independent power

of ministers, making them completely subservient to the king and the cabal.

The one remaining check on the power of the cabal was Parliament, and this had been nullified by skillful use of the "influence" which was at the disposal of the crown through its power to control honors, patronage, and peerages. This influence, Burke says, "converted the very antagonist into the instrument of power." Burke sees no hope except through the willingness of public-spirited and uncorrupted men to stand together to preserve the constitution and, as a last resort, "the interposition of the body of the people itself." "If other ideas should prevail," he concludes, "things must remain in their present confusion; until they are hurried into all the rage of civil violence; or until they sink into the dead repose of despotism."

Walpole, like Burke, believed that English freedom was endangered by a determined, cunning, and well-calculated plan to increase the power of the crown, but, unlike Burke, he viewed the problem as a matter of personalities rather than methods. Walpole attributes to the king's mother and Lord Bute the origins of that fatal ambition which was to have such disastrous consequences. "It must, I think, appear evident," Walpole writes, "from the scope of the reign, that the Princess Dowager and Lord Bute had assumed the reins with a fixed intention of raising the prerogative, which they called restoring it to its ancient lustre." Walpole does not hold George III responsible for the first steps taken in this plan. When the reign began the young king appeared to be "humane and benevolent" and unfailingly courteous, although showing signs of "that cool dissimulation in which he had been so well initiated by his mother." To Walpole, the dominant feature of his early years was his indolence and his dependence on Bute. "He resigned himself obsequiously to the government of his mother and Lord Bute," Walpole writes, "learned, and even entered with art into the lessons they inspired, but added nothing of his own. When the task was done, he relapsed into indifference and indolence till roused to the next day's part."

The original objectives of the Princess and Bute, in Walpole's opinion, were modest, being directed at "humbling the aristocracy, rather than invading Liberty." Walpole concedes that this undertaking was not without justification, and he blames the Duke of Newcastle, Henry Pelham and Lord Hardwicke for provoking it by their own high-handed behavior. Once the first step had been taken, however, ambition began to swell. "Let it be observed," Walpole adds, "that, when I impute to the King and his mother little more than a formed design to reducing the usurped authority of the great Lords, I am far from meaning that there were not deeper designs at bottom." These deeper designs turn out to be something like Burke's cabal, a body of politicians who saw an opportunity to advance their authoritarian views. These include Lord Mansfield ("by principle a tyrant"), Lord Holland ("bred in a monarchic school"), George Grenville ("bold, proud, dictatorial"), the Duke of Bedford's faction ("void of honour, honesty, and virtue"), and the Scotch ("whatever their masters wished them to be"). "All these individuals or factions," Walpole asserts, "I do not doubt, accepted and fomented the disposition they found predominant in the Cabinet."

From these beginnings Walpole traces the progressive corruption of a young king, whose inherent love of power was strengthened by his mother, cultivated by his tutor, encouraged by ambitious politicians, and eventually fanned into flame by opposition. "Thus on the innate desire of unbounded power in all princes," Walpole says, "was engrafted a hate to the freedom of the subject, and therefore whether the King set out with a plan of extending his prerogative, or adopted it, his later measures, as often as he had an opportunity of directing them himself, tended to the sole object of acting by his own will." The consequences were the inevitable result of ambition and pride. "Frequent convul-

sions did that pursuit occasion," Walpole observes, "and heavy mortifications to himself. On the nation it heaped disgrace, and brought it to the brink of ruin; and should the event be consonant to the King's wishes of establishing the royal authority at home, it is more sure that the country will be so lowered, that the Sovereign will become as subject to the mandates of France, as any little potentate in Europe."

II. THE WHIG HISTORIANS

By the middle years of the reign of Queen Victoria an interpretation of the reign of George III had emerged which was long the dominant one and which is still firmly embedded in many encyclopedias and textbooks. The outstanding examples of this "Whig Interpretation" are the works of Thomas Erskine May and W. E. H. Lecky. These men viewed the reign of George III from the standpoint of mid-Victorian liberalism, and they judged men or events by the extent to which they advanced or impeded the evolution of the parliamentary institutions of their own time. To May and Lecky the principal feature of the reigns of George I and George II was the evolution of government by cabinet responsible to parliament. In the reign of George III they saw a last desperate effort to stem the tide of constitutionalism and restore an independent power to the crown. In their view George III, despite extenuating circumstances, was at worst an embryo tyrant whom history had foiled, and at best a deluded man who had set his face against the march of progress. George III was judged, not by standards of his own age, but by standards developed a century later. In the telling phrase of Romney Sedgwick, "by a double distortion he has been represented as having endeavoured to imitate the Stuarts when he ought to have anticipated Queen Victoria." [2]

May and Lecky treat the problem in similar fashion, although in style May is direct and unqualified while Lecky intro-

[2] See page 57.

duces many qualifications. On the question of the intentions of George III they both agree that he began his reign with a determination to strengthen the power of the crown, but a difference in emphasis is apparent. Characteristically, May states his point in emphatic terms: "The king desired to undertake personally the chief administration of public affairs, to direct the power of his ministers, and himself to distribute the patronage of the crown. He was ambitious not only to reign, but to govern. . . . He came to the throne determined to exalt the kingly office; and throughout his reign he never lost sight of that paramount object." Lecky makes the same point, but in extenuation he admits that in 1760 "this design was in many respects more plausible than is now generally admitted," and he concedes that "it is probable that Burke, in the famous pamphlet in which he described the condition of English politics in the first years of George III, considerably exaggerated the systematic and elaborate character of the plan that was adopted." Lecky also recites some of the arguments which were advanced at the time in support of such a plan, and he points out that George III would be supported in such an undertaking by the teachings of the law and the church and the concurrence of a strong body of public opinion.

May and Lecky agree in assigning to George III energy, determination, and commendable personal qualities. Again, it is May who is the more straightforward and blunt. "The king," he states, "was naturally ambitious, and delighted in the active exercise of power." At the same time he concedes, with some admiration and respect, that the king displayed piety, constancy, and patriotism. Compared with May's straightforward assessments of praise and blame, Lecky's treatment of George III has a carping quality. Lecky emphasizes the negative features of his personality: he was dominated by his mother; "he exhibited during his whole career the characteristic merits and defects of a female

education;" he was "always singularly deficient in literary culture;" and while he was scrupulous, dutiful, and sincerely pious, he was also harsh in his judgment of others, prejudiced, obstinate, tenacious of resentments, and sullen. His indolence he overcame by an effort of will, "but the other lines of this not very pleasing picture continued during his whole life."

On the question of the relation of the king to his ministers, both May and Lecky assume that in the reigns of George I and George II a system of government had emerged which was marked by the responsibility of ministers to Parliament. May states this proposition unequivocally: "The government of the state was conducted, throughout all its departments, by ministers responsible to Parliament for every act of their administration . . . and who resigned when their advice was disregarded by the crown, or their policy disapproved by Parliament. . . . The king reigned, but his ministers governed." Lecky begins his account of the reign of George III with a disquisition on the advantages of cabinet government as it had evolved in England, but he qualifies these remarks with the statement that "in the eighteenth century the Whig ideal was still far from its attainment," and he points out that "the conception of the cabinet as a body of statesmen who were in thorough political agreement, and were jointly responsible for all the measures they proposed, was still in its early stage, and was by no means fully or universally recognized."

Both May and Lecky emphasize that George III attempted to make ministers responsible solely to his own will. "The young king, George III," May states, "on succeeding to the throne, regarded with settled jealousy the power of his ministers, as an encroachment on his own, and resolved to break it down. . . . The king desired to undertake personally the chief administration of public affairs, to direct the policy of his ministers, and himself to distribute the patronage of the crown." Both May and Lecky stress the importance of a change in the structure of political parties to accomplish this end. Both agree that George III undermined the independent powers of parliamentary leaders by breaking up the Whig groups, thus rendering their leaders impotent, and by building a party of Tories and "king's friends" which would support the independence and power of the crown.

To May and Lecky, however, the most damning quality of George III was that he attempted to block those constitutional developments which resulted in cabinet government in a parliamentary system. May represents George III as attempting to return to the past: "to revert to a polity under which kings had governed, and ministers had executed their orders, was in itself a dangerous retrogression in the principles of constitutional government." Lecky's criticism was that he was not on the side of the future — that he attempted to carry English government in a direction which the course of history had rejected. "Ignorant, narrow-minded and arbitrary," Lecky states, "with an unbounded confidence in his own judgment and an extravagant estimate of his prerogative, resolved at all hazards to compel his ministers to adopt his own views, or to undermine them if they refused, he spent a long life in obstinately resisting measures which are now almost universally admitted to have been good, and in supporting measures which are as universally admitted to have been bad."

III. THE NAMIER SCHOOL

In the historiography of the reign of George III, the work of Sir Lewis Namier may be said to mark the beginning of the modern period. Namier's major contribution was an analysis of the "structure" of politics in the early years of the reign of George III. His acute and detailed research revealed a political world far different from that of his own day and far different from that which the Whig historians had conceived. Namier struck a powerful blow against the Whig interpretation of

history in two important respects. First, he insisted that eighteenth century kings and politicians must be understood and evaluated within the framework of politics of their own time and that this understanding of the period could be achieved only after an exhaustive examination of the evidence. Secondly, he denied the contention that broad questions of constitutional principle were important in shaping political action, finding his explanations of the political process in the ambitions and actions of individuals seeking their own advantage. Thus, he denied the validity of the view that the early years of the reign of George III must be understood as involving a major constitutional conflict.

Namier's argument rests on two related points. One is that there was a well-established consensus concerning the powers of the crown in the English constitutional system. He raises the question: "Can we find in the first ten years of George III's reign a real, fundamental difference of ideas concerning the nature and extent of Royal power . . . ?" His answer to this question is "no." "In reality," Namier insists, "the constitutional practice of George III differed little from that of George I and George II." The constitutional questions which were raised by the opposition he regards as empty rhetoric used to serve the immediate and personal interests of politicians. The alleged constitutional issue he finds to have been unreal — it was invented by later historians to fill a gap in the constitutional theory of the time with "conceptions belonging to a later age."

The second point in Namier's refutation of the great constitutional issue raised by the Whig historians is his denial that George III had either the desire or the ability to alter the existing and accepted role of the crown. "But was he ambitious?" Namier asks. "Did he try to exercise powers which his predecessors had relinquished, or claim an influence which was not universally conceded to him?" Again Namier's answer is "no." George III, he says, was too ineffectual — too tied up in emotional knots — to have undertaken a systematic effort to extend the power of the crown, or if he had, he was too incapable to have met with the degree of success which the Whig historians had claimed for him. In his essay "King George III: A Study of Personality" Namier describes George III as his letters reveal him — "warts and all," rejecting "the stories circulated about him by very clever and eloquent contemporaries" and the "injurious legend which made that heavy-burdened man a much maligned ruler." It is Namier's contention that such a man could not be the able, unscrupulous, power-seeking king of Whig historiography.

In his lecture "The King and His Ministers" Namier argues that the Whig historians had based their interpretation of George III on a misunderstanding of eighteenth-century politics. He denies that under George I and George II a system of government had emerged by which ministers were responsible to Parliament. In the eighteenth century, he says, the king was expected to act as the chief executive, and ministers were primarily responsible to him. He stresses the doctrine of the independence of the king in choosing his ministers, although he concedes that this freedom was severely restricted by the small number of men of ministerial calibre. The other great error of the Whig historians, in Namier's view, was to assume the existence of strong political parties upon which a cabinet system of government could rest. Namier emphasizes the lack of party organization in the House of Commons, where "probably less than half thought and acted in party terms." Under such circumstances cabinet government was impossible and the king would necessarily be thrust into a position of personal responsibility.

Not the least of the contributions of Sir Lewis Namier was to inspire other historians with his own concern for the history of the reign of George III and his own rigorous methods of historical research. Romney Sedgwick's *Letters of George III to Lord Bute* is an important product of the Namier school. In the introduction to this volume Sedgwick points out that in the eighteenth century the heir to the throne was invariably the center of opposition to the reigning monarch and his ministers, and that this "Leicester House opposition" invariably adopted vague plans of reform which appealed to discontented elements in parliament and in the country. George III, Sedgwick says, followed the usual pattern when he spoke about reformations and freeing the crown from ministerial tyranny, but Sedgwick treats these statements as the conventional cries of opposition, doomed to be discarded once power was achieved. "Such slogans had no more practical significance in 1760 than in 1727 or 1788," he states. The changes in political climate which accompanied the accession of George III are to be explained, not on the basis of theoretical plans of reform, but as growing out of a new political situation, dominated by the lack of an heir around whom the opposition could gather. Lacking such a reversionary hope, opposition spokesmen such as Burke could only take refuge in a high constitutional line against the power of the crown. Thus Sedgwick, like Namier, believes that a proper understanding of eighteenth century politics reduces the supposed innovations of George III and Bute to the dimensions of a tempest in a teapot. Those changes which do appear are not the result of a conscious effort to change the direction of constitutional development, but are the normal and expected features of the politics of the time. "There is nothing to add," Sedgwick states, "to this explanation of that so-called 'break in the smooth development of our constitutional history' which, according to the familiar legend, was due to 'the able attempt of George III to recover the powers of the crown. . . .'"

IV. THE RESPONSE TO NAMIER

Contemporary scholarship on the reign of George III may be described as an attempt to come to terms with Namier.

Some historians have surrendered uncon-ditionally; others have tried to defend certain isolated positions; and others have counter-attacked with vigor. None has denied that Namier's work has given strong impetus to new thinking and new research and has made untenable certain aspects of the old interpretations.

The work of Richard Pares represents one response to Namier. Pares' interpretation of George III reveals the extent to which modern historians have profited from Namier's work, but it also shows a man of independent judgment who refuses to accept all of Namier's views at face value. Pares denies Namier's contention that George III followed in the path of his predecessor. He raises the question: "If George III only did what George II had done, why did the politicians suddenly make a fuss about it?" His answer is that George III did attempt innovations at the beginning of his reign, but that these were innovations of practice rather than of principle. Pares takes a more favorable attitude toward George III's abilities; the "warts" in his personality are not allowed to obscure his more substantial qualities, especially his efforts to advance professionalism in government. On the question of the relation of the king and his ministers, Pares warns against the rigid, legalistic interpretation of the Namier school. A valid constitutional question could arise, Pares states, because the personal role of the king in the determination of policy and selection of ministers was ill-defined. George III, Pares asserts, attempted to make his personal wishes more effective in this area than George II had done, and thus aroused controversy with the opposition, who sought to define his powers in this respect very narrowly. In the works of Richard Pares the student will find a judicious, well-reasoned approach to the problems of the reign of George III.

A more direct attack on the interpretations of Sir Lewis Namier has been launched by W. R. Fryer, who has attempted to salvage some of the viewpoints of the Whig historians. Fryer rejects the extreme Whig view that George III showed inclinations toward high-prerogative government, but he also rejects the Namier view that George III was acting essentially in the same way as his predecessor. It is Fryer's contention that while George III adhered scrupulously to law and legal forms he encroached upon many "constitutional usages and proprieties" in ways which would make him a more powerful and active king than George II had been. George III, Fryer maintains, "repeatedly acted in a manner contrary to the constitutional duties of a monarch of his age." "He did so . . . not indeed by breaking any law; but by ignoring certain conventions of behaviour which had every claim on his respect." Like Pares, Fryer insists that the limitations on the power of an eighteenth century monarch should be sought in the practical realities of politics as well as in legal prescriptions. Chief among these was the existence of ultimate power in the house of commons and the need for the king to appoint ministers and follow policies which the House of Commons would approve. The unwillingness of George III to accept these practical limitations, in Fryer's opinion, is the basis for the charge that he acted unconstitutionally. While Fryer concedes that the Whig historians of the last century misstated and over-stated their case, he returns to the view expressed by Burke in 1770, that the policy of the crown "without directly violating the letter of the law, operates against the spirit of the whole constitution."

Fryer also rejects Sir Lewis Namier's low opinion of the abilities of George III. Namier, he says, saw many of George III's weaknesses, but failed to see certain elements of strength. "It is difficult to resist the impression," Fryer says, "that he had always been, in some ways, a more positive character than Sir Lewis seems to allow . . . and that these more positive characteristics of his had been making a considerable contribution to politics in other ways than the expression of obstinacy and fixed ideas." Furthermore, he had the capacity to grow with experience. "The King who could be, and do, all this," Fryer states, "had certainly become, or perhaps we should say revealed, a character considerably different from the estimate which Sir Lewis Namier gave us. He had revealed himself as no more profound or an original mind than Sir Lewis represented him; perhaps not even as, at bottom, a more self-confident one. But he had shown himself a far more forceful and dominant one; as a man deserving, despite all his limitations, the description of formidable, and even, in a real sense, of ambitious."

Herbert Butterfield has attacked both the Whig historians and the Namier school. His *The Whig Interpretation of History* examines the tendency to write history from the perspective of the present "and to produce a story which is the ratification, if not the glorification of the present." Although not directed against the Whig historians of the reign of George III (most of the examples are drawn from the Reformation), the ideas expressed are clearly applicable to the works of May and Lecky. In his *George III and the Historians* Butterfield presents in detail the case against the Whig historians of George III.

Having settled with the Whig historians Butterfield turns his guns against the interpretations of Sir Lewis Namier and his followers. In his approach to the problem Butterfield returns to the old "Tory interpretation" of Adolphus, which held that George III had attempted a change of system at his accession, and that this change was constitutionally justifiable. He rejects the contention of the Whig historians that George III attempted to block the development of cabinet government, and he also rejects Sir Lewis Namier's view that George III attempted no significant changes in the role of the monarch. Butterfield holds that there is abundant evidence that George III began his reign with the intention of making important changes in the role of the crown and that his actions provoked an important constitutional conflict. In Butterfield's view the question was not cabinet government, which did not exist in the form in which the Whig historians had conceived it, but something important at that time. It was what George III and his advisers said it was: to free himself from dependence on the Whig aristocracy and to bring an end to corruption in Parliament and elections. And, Butterfield states, this was a policy which would evoke widespread approval.

Butterfield's criticism of the Namier interpretation rests on three major points: that Sir Lewis Namier interpreted too rigidly the right of the king to choose his ministers; that he underestimated the importance of political parties; and that he failed to recognize the importance of ideas in shaping the actions of the king. Butterfield argues that although the right of the king to choose his ministers was legally unimpeachable, practical necessities greatly circumscribed this right. Butterfield also takes issue with Sir Lewis Namier's interpretation of the role and nature of political parties. Although political parties in the modern sense did not exist, there were political groupings which could command formidable power and which would carry great weight in the formation of ministries or the determination of policy.

Finally, while applauding the thoroughness of research which characterizes Sir Lewis Namier's work, Butterfield states that Namier's method has caused him to lose sight of the intangibles which are part of any political situation. "It is in the minds of the men concerned —," Butterfield writes, "in the continuity of their reflection and their purposes — that history acquires a coherence and cohesion, instead of presenting a mere chaos of chances and conjunctures, cross-currents and inconsistencies. The story gains meaning only through that framework of ideas and purposes within which men act even when they seem only to be responding casually to circumstances. . . ." Failure to recognize the importance of ideas in history has, in Butterfield's opinion, led Sir Lewis Namier astray. "Focussing itself so exclusively on the mechanics of political action, the Namier interpretation refuses to see any serious conflict of ideas, any serious political issues, in the events of the years 1760–3, the age of Bute. . . . The troubles of the early years of George III's reign, says Sir Lewis Namier, were due to little things, to muddles and jealousies, and to ludicrous ironies of circumstance." This view Butterfield strongly denies. He insists it ignores a great body of evidence that George III did have plans for important changes. "George III did have strong ideas about the government of the country," Butterfield says, "and particularly about the role of the king. Indeed, he held some of them with such consistency, that his attachment to them has been one of the reasons for regarding him as an obstinate man."

After studying the competing and often contradictory interpretations expressed in these selections, the student should see that the question "Tyrant or Constitutional Monarch?" fails to do justice to the complexity of the problem. Each historian has seen the problem in his own way, but in so doing he has formulated new questions and offered new answers. From the crude, two-dimensional, partisan statements of Wraxall and Adolphus, Burke and Wal-

pole, through the detailed but often unhistorical interpretations of May and Lecky, historical understanding has advanced to the sophisticated, complex, subtly shaded interpretations of today. We now see that there are further depths to be plumbed in the never-ending effort to understand this important period of English history.

Such a study should be more than an academic exercise. We may hope that the study of the reign of George III will bring a wisdom much needed in our own lives and our own times. The following words of Herbert Butterfield, although not applied by him to the reign of George III, could serve as a guide to students of this complex and controversial period: "Studying the quarrels of an ancient day [the historian] can at least seek to understand both parties to the struggle and he must want to understand them better than they understood themselves; watching them entangled in the net of time and circumstance he can take pity on them — these men who perhaps had no pity for one another; and, though he can never be perfect, it is difficult to see why he should aspire to anything less than taking these men and their quarrels into a world where everything is understood and all sins are forgiven." [3]

[3] Herbert Butterfield, *The Whig Interpretation of History* (New York, 1951), p. 3.

CHRONOLOGICAL TABLE

1714	Accession of George I
1721–42	Ministry of Robert Walpole
1727	Accession of George II
1738	Birth of George III
1742–43	Wilmington Ministry
1743–54	Newcastle–Pelham Ministry
1751	Death of Frederick Louis, Prince of Wales
1754–56	Newcastle Ministry
1756–57	Devonshire–Pitt Ministry
1757	Formation of Newcastle–Pitt Ministry
1760	Death of George II; accession of George III (October)
1761	Bute made Secretary of State (March)
1761	Resignation of Pitt (October)
1762	Resignation of Newcastle (May)
1762	Bute Ministry formed (May)
1762	Henry Fox made leader of the House of Commons (October)
1762	Debate on the Peace; Treaty approved by both houses (December)
1763	Resignation of Bute (April)
1763–65	Grenville Ministry
1765–66	Rockingham Ministry
1766–68	Chatham Ministry
1768–70	Grafton Ministry
1770–82	North Ministry
1782	Rockingham Ministry
1782–83	Shelburne Ministry
1783	Portland Ministry (Fox–North Coalition)
1783–1801	Ministry of William Pitt the Younger
1820	Death of George III

THE PRINCIPAL PROPER NAMES
Appearing in the Readings

AUGUSTA OF SAXE-GOTHA, PRINCESS OF WALES: *wife of Frederick Louis, Prince of Wales; mother of George III.*

BATH, EARL OF: *see William Pulteney.*

BEDFORD, JOHN RUSSELL, 4TH DUKE OF: *great nobleman with a small but important party in the house of commons; ambassador to negotiate peace, 1762–63.*

BLACKSTONE, SIR WILLIAM: *jurist famous for his* Commentaries on the Laws of England.

BOLINGBROKE, HENRY SAINT-JOHN, 1ST VISCOUNT: *a Tory leader under Queen Anne; opponent of Robert Walpole; author of* The Patriot King *and other political works.*

BUTE, JOHN STUART, 3RD EARL OF: *tutor and confidant of George III; Secretary of State, 1761–62; First Lord of the Treasury, 1762–63; after his resignation in 1763 was increasingly excluded from influence by the jealousy of ministers; by 1766 his influence with George III had ended.*

CAROLINE OF ANSBACH, QUEEN OF GEORGE II: *an intelligent, forceful queen who exercised important influence over George II; a strong supporter of Robert Walpole.*

CARTERET, JOHN, EARL GRANVILLE: *favorite of George I and George II; rival and opponent of Robert Walpole; failed to form a ministry with Bath in 1746, after which his influence waned.*

CHARLOTTE OF MECKLENBURG-STRELITZ, QUEEN OF GEORGE III: *a submissive queen who did not interfere in political matters; absorbed in her household and large family.*

CHATHAM, EARL OF: *see William Pitt.*

CONWAY, HENRY SEYMOUR: *soldier and politician; friend of Horace Walpole; dismissed from office in 1764 for opposing the Grenville ministry; held various offices in subsequent ministries.*

CUMBERLAND, WILLIAM AUGUSTUS, DUKE OF: *second and favorite son of George II; followed a military career; instrumental in forming the first Rockingham ministry, 1765–66.*

DEVONSHIRE, WILLIAM CAVENDISH, 4TH DUKE OF: *head of a great landed family; nominal head of the ministry in alliance with Pitt, 1756–57; his connection with Newcastle after Newcastle's resignation led to dismissal from his office as Lord Chamberlain in 1762.*

DODINGTON, GEORGE BUBB, BARON MELCOMBE: *friend and adviser of Frederick Louis, Prince of Wales and the Princess Augusta; noted for his* Diary.

FOX, CHARLES JAMES: *son of Henry Fox; a leader of the opposition to Lord North and the American war; Secretary of State in the Rockingham (1782) and Portland (1783) ministries; after 1783 leader of opposition to the younger Pitt.*

FOX, HENRY, 1ST BARON HOLLAND: *rival of the elder William Pitt; leader of the house of commons under Bute, 1762–63.*

FREDERICK LOUIS, PRINCE OF WALES: *eldest son of George II and father of George III; usually a center of opposition to George II and his ministers.*

GERMAIN, LORD GEORGE SACKVILLE: *disgraced in 1759 for insubordination at the battle of Minden; Colonial Secretary, 1775–82; held principal responsibility for management of the American war.*

GRAFTON, AUGUSTUS HENRY FITZROY, 3RD DUKE OF: *Secretary of State in Rockingham ministry, 1765–66; nominal head of Chatham administration, 1766–68; headed the ministry, 1768–70; resigned office in 1775 in opposition to the American war; member of Rockingham ministry, 1782.*

GRANVILLE, EARL: *see Carteret.*

GRENVILLE, GEORGE: *First Lord of the Treasury, 1763–65; alienated George III by his jealousy of Bute and his insistence on full and open support; principal events of his ministry were the prosecution of Wilkes and the Stamp Act.*

HARDWICKE, PHILIP YORKE, 1ST EARL OF: *Lord Chancellor, 1737–1756; adviser and close friend of Newcastle.*

HOLLAND, LORD: *see Henry Fox.*

JOHNSON, SAMUEL: *literary leader of his time; best known for his English Dictionary; a staunch Tory and strong supporter of George III.*

JUNIUS: *pen name of a pamphleteer who attacked George III and his ministers in a brilliant series of letters, 1769–72; usually identified as Philip Francis, then a clerk in the War Office.*

MANSFIELD, WILLIAM MURRAY, 1ST EARL OF: *Scottish lawyer and politician; Lord Chief Justice, 1756–88; supported the court and the American war.*

MELCOMBE, BARON: *see George Bubb Dodington.*

NEWCASTLE, THOMAS PELHAM-HOLLES, 1ST DUKE OF: *with his brother (Henry Pelham) dominated politics from the fall of Walpole to 1756; joined with Pitt in 1757 in a ministry which won great successes in the Seven Years War; after the accession of George III the jealousies and rivalries of Bute, Newcastle and Pitt led to Newcastle's resignation in 1762.*

NORTH, FREDERICK: *First Lord of the Treasury, 1770–82; lack of success in the American war brought his downfall in 1782; offended George III in 1783 by returning to office under Portland in coalition with Charles James Fox.*

PELHAM, HENRY: *brother of Duke of Newcastle; First Lord of the Treasury from 1743 until his death in 1754.*

PORTLAND, WILLIAM HENRY CAVENDISH BENTINCK, 3RD DUKE OF: *head of a great landed family; politically and socially connected with the Rockingham group; headed the ministry in 1783 and 1807–09.*

PITT, WILLIAM, EARL OF CHATHAM: *great leader during the Seven Years War; resigned in 1761 and opposed the peace treaty of 1763; as Lord Chatham headed an unsuccessful ministry from 1766–68; opposed the American policy of North.*

PITT, WILLIAM, "THE YOUNGER": *son of Chatham; First Lord of the Treasury, 1783–1801 and 1804–06.*

PULTENEY, WILLIAM, EARL OF BATH: *a leading opponent of Robert Walpole; his influence waned after 1746.*

ROCKINGHAM, CHARLES WATSON-WENTWORTH, 2ND MARQUIS OF: *headed ministry (1765–66) which repealed the Stamp Act; a leader of opposition to Lord North and the American war; formed second ministry in 1782 which opened negotiations for peace; ministry terminated after three months by his death.*

SANDWICH, JOHN MONTAGU, 4TH EARL OF: *Secretary of State in Grenville ministry, 1763–65; First Lord of the Admiralty under North, 1771–82; retired from public life after fall of North ministry in 1782.*

SECKER, THOMAS: *archbishop of Canterbury, 1758–1768.*

STONE, ANDREW: *secretary to Duke of Newcastle; became Treasurer to Queen Charlotte in 1761 and attached himself to the court.*

WALDEGRAVE, JAMES, 2ND EARL WALDEGRAVE: *trusted friend and confidant of George II; governor of the Prince of Wales (later George III); noted for his memoirs.*

WALPOLE, SIR ROBERT: *First Lord of the Treasury, 1721–42; support of George II and Queen Caroline and his parliamentary and administrative ability enabled him to dominate politics until his fall in 1742.*

WILKES, JOHN: *political adventurer who acme to prominence by his attacks on Bute in 1762–63; in exile from 1763–68; elected to parliament in 1768 but rejected by the house of commons; elected and took his seat in 1774; made his career by appealing to London radicalism.*

The Conflict of Opinion

"That he committed many errors, nourished many prejudices, formed many erroneous estimates, and frequently adhered too pertinaciously to his determinations, where he conceived, perhaps falsely, that they were founded in reason or in justice — all these allegations may be admitted. But all these infirmities, from which no man is exempt, cannot impugn his right to the affectionate veneration of posterity for the inflexible uprightness of his public conduct. . . ."

— Nathanial Wraxall

"I can without hesitation declare my opinion, that, in the period on which I have written, the throne has been filled by a monarch who has sought the love of his subjects through the means of public spirit and private virtue; and who has tempered a noble desire to preserve from degradation the authority he inherits, with a firm and just regard to the constitution and liberties which conducted him to the throne, and which will ever form its best supports."

— John Adolphus

"His Majesty came to the throne of these kingdoms with more advantages than any of his predecessors since the Revolution. . . . These singular advantages inspired his Majesty only with a more ardent desire to preserve unimpaired the spirit of that national freedom to which he owed a situation so full of glory. But to others it suggested sentiments of a very different nature. They thought they beheld an opportunity . . . of drawing to themselves, by the aggrandizement of a court faction, a degree of power which they could never hope to derive from natural influence or from honourable service. . . . The discretionary power of the crown in the formation of ministry, abused by bad or weak men, has given rise to a system, which without directly violating the letter of any law, operates against the spirit of the whole constitution."

—Edmund Burke

"No British monarch has ascended the throne with so many advantages as George the Third. . . . A passionate, domineering woman, and a Favourite without talents, soon drew a cloud over this shining prospect. . . . The views of the Court were so fully manifested afterwards, that no doubt can be entertained but a plan had been early formed of carrying the prerogative to very unusual heights. . . ."

— Horace Walpole

"The king desired to undertake personally the chief administration of public affairs, to direct the policy of his ministers, and himself to distribute the patronage of the crown. He was ambitious not only to reign, but to govern. His will was strong and resolute, his courage high, and his talent for intrigue considerable. He came to the throne determined to exalt the kingly office; and throughout his long reign he never lost sight of that paramount object."

— Thomas Erskine May

"All these things have contributed very naturally to throw a delusive veil over the political errors of a sovereign of whom it may be said without exaggeration, that he inflicted more profound and enduring injuries upon his country than any other modern English king. . . . The root, however, of his great errors lay in his determination to restore the royal power to a position wholly different from that which it occupied in the reign of his predecessor. . . .

— W. E. H. Lecky

"I have given here a picture of George III as seen in his letters, 'warts and all.' What I have never been able to find is the man arrogating power to himself, the ambitious schemer out to dominate, the intriguer dealing in an underhand fashion with his Ministers; in short, any evidence for the stories circulated about him by very clever and eloquent contemporaries. He had a high, indeed an exaggerated, notion of royalty but in terms of mission and duties rather than of power; and trying to live up to this idealized concept, he made unreasonable demands on himself. He himself did not understand the nature and depth of his tragedy; still less could others. There was therefore room for the growth of an injurious legend which made that heavy-burdened man a much maligned ruler; and which has long been accepted as history."

— Sir Lewis Namier

"George III's behaviour as Prince of Wales must be regarded as a typical example of the normal political life-cycle of the eighteenth-century heir-apparent; . . . the exceptional feature of the first twenty years of his reign was the absence, not of 'responsible government,' which had never existed, but of the reversionary factor."

— Romney Sedgwick

"George III did try to restore something which possibly ought to have existed, but did not exist, when he came to the throne. He did what George II ought to have done, rather than what George II had done. . . ."

— Richard Pares

"Let us grant, as fully as possible, that there is no case whatever for presenting the King as an enemy of the constitution, as embodied in law.
Let us grant that we must firmly resist any temptation to judge the King's
career by standards of constitutional propriety not proper to the age in
which he lived. It does not follow that Sir Lewis Namier's account of his
career is an adequate one. I wish to suggest . . . that George III repeatedly
acted in a manner contrary to the constitutional duties of a monarch of his
own age. . . ."

— W. R. FRYER

"When we come to the year 1760, shall we say that a change of system
occurred, though we know that complications will have to be introduced
into the story when we examine it in detail?. . . . The answer to the decisive question depends on what George III, Bute and their collaborators
had in mind, behind the chaos of contradictions, cross-purposes and tactical
moves. . . . It is in the minds of the men concerned — in the continuity
of their reflection and their purpose — that history acquires a coherence
and cohesion, instead of presenting a mere chaos of chances and conjunctures, cross-currents and inconsistencies. . . ."

— HERBERT BUTTERFIELD

I. CONTEMPORARY VIEWS

The Man of Good Intentions

NATHANIAL WRAXALL

Nathanial Wraxall (1751–1831) was a traveller and professional man of letters, who sat in Parliament from 1780–1794, usually supporting the court. His *Historical Memoirs* were first published in 1815, and immediately became popular. His favorable portrayal of George III derives from the outlook of one who sought favor and advancement from the court and whose knowledge of George III was based on that king's mature and most effective years. Although the historical accuracy of the memoirs has been severely criticized, Wraxall shows a good knowledge of the men who were active in the middle decades of the reign of George III, and his memoirs are valuable for their vivid character sketches of prominent and less prominent persons in politics and society.

Perhaps no portion of time in the course of the two last centuries offers, proportionably to its duration, so few of those interesting anecdotes where the sovereign comes personally forward to our inspection as the reign of George III. The reason is obvious, and arose out of the King's character. Charles II and Louis XIV, surrounded by mistresses and all the dissipation of a court, presented to Burnet, to Grammont, or to Voltaire perpetual matter of entertaining recital. Even George I and George II offered some resources of a similar nature to Lord Melcomb for his "Diary," and to Horace Walpole for his "Reminiscences." But his present Majesty's whole life, from the age of twenty-two down to the period at which he ceased to reign, was passed either in the severe and exemplary discharge of his *public* duties of every description, according to his conception of them, or in the bosom of his family, amidst *domestic* sources of amusement. In his agricultural occupations, or when engaged in the diversions of the field,

he was only seen by a few individuals, who from their official situations or dignity had access to his person. No splendid assemblies of both sexes, or festive entertainments to which beauty, rank, and pleasure, in a comprehensive sense, must have contributed, by levelling him in some measure with his guests, presented him to view divested of the forms of royalty. Unlike his predecessor, who even at an advanced age still preserved a relish for those enjoyments, equally unlike his son, the present Regent, whose graceful manners and love of social enjoyment, cemented by wine and conversation, have rendered his palace the centre of pleasures, George III, while young, neither frequented masquerades, nor ever engaged at play, nor protracted the hours of convivial festivity, nor passed his evenings in company calculated to unbend his mind from the fatigues of business and vexations of state.

All the splendour of a court was laid aside, or only exhibited for a few hours on a birthday. Rarely during the first

From Nathanial W. Wraxall, *The Historical and Posthumous Memoirs of Sir Nathanial William Wraxall, 1772–1784,* ed. by Henry B. Wheatley, 5 vols. (London, 1884), vol. I, pp. 6–8, 279–287, 302–306.

twenty years after his accession did he join in any scene of public amusement, if we except the diversion of the theatre. Still more rarely did he sit down at table with any of his courtiers or nobility. His repasts, private, short, and temperate, never led to the slightest excess. Hence his enemies endeavoured to represent him, most unjustly, as affecting the state of an Asiatic prince, scarcely ever visible except on the terrace at Windsor or in the circle at a levee. "Junius," who saw him through the most unfavourable medium, and who converted his very virtues into subjects of accusation or of reproach, pictures St. James's as a court "where prayers are morality, and kneeling is religion." It was not till a period later than the point of time at which these Memoirs stop that the King began to mix in a select company, and occasionally to indulge in the pleasures of society. Previous to the year 1784, it is only in the foreign or domestic transactions of his reign, often only within the walls of one or the other House of Parliament, that the materials can generally be found for writing the internal history of the time.

*   *   *

He was born in Norfolk House, St. James's Square, where Frederick, Prince of Wales, then resided, who had been peremptorily ordered only a short time before to quit St. James's Palace by George II. I saw, not much more than a year ago, the identical bed in which the Prince was born, now removed to the Duke of Norfolk's seat of Worksop, in the county of Nottingham; and it forcibly proves the rapid progress of domestic elegance and taste within the last eighty years. Except that the furniture is of green silk, the bed has nothing splendid about it, and would hardly be esteemed fit for the accommodation of a person of ordinary condition in the present times. A course of systematic abstinence and exercise had secured to George III the enjoyment of almost uninterrupted health down to the time of

which I speak. So little had he been incommoded by sickness or by indisposition of any kind from the period of his accession till his memorable seizure in 1788, that scarcely was he ever compelled to absent himself on that account from a levée, a council, or a drawing-room during eight-and-twenty years. One only exception to this remark occurred in the autumn of 1765, when he was attacked by a disorder that confined him for several weeks; relative to the nature and seat of which malady, though many conjectures and assertions have been hazarded in conversation, and even in print, no satisfactory information has ever been given to the world.

In the King's countenance a physiognomist would have distinguished two principal characteristics: firmness, or, as his enemies denominated it, obstinacy, tempered with benignity. The former expression was, however, indisputably more marked and prominent than the latter sentiment. Fox, when addressing the House of Commons, did not hesitate to allude in very intelligible language to his obstinacy. I remember, in January 1782, on his moving for papers in order to institute an inquiry into Lord Sandwich's conduct at the head of the Admiralty, Fox observed, "It is said by the very members of this assembly who, in case of a division, will vote in favour of the Earl of Sandwich, that there is *an obstinacy somewhere* which will oppose whatever measure is suggested from this side of the House. . . . I cannot pretend to say whether such *a spirit of obstinacy* does or does not exist, but those men who really think the present First Lord of the Admiralty unfit for his situation, and yet come down to vote for maintaining him in office, are unfit for the important trust of representatives of a free people." I believe there was no person present so obtuse as not to understand the application of Fox's expressions. The King seemed to have a tendency to become corpulent, if he had not repressed it by habitual and unremitting temperance. On this subject I shall relate a fact which was communicated to me by a friend, Sir John Macpherson, who received it from the great Earl of Mansfield, to whom the King himself mentioned it, forcibly demonstrating that strength of mind, renunciation of all excesses, and dominion over his appetites, which have characterised George III at every period of his life. Conversing with William, Duke of Cumberland, his uncle, not long before that Prince's death, in 1765, his Majesty observed that it was with concern he remarked the Duke's augmenting corpulency. "I lament it not less, sir," replied he, "but it is constitutional, and I am much mistaken if your Majesty will not become as large as myself before you attain to my age." "It arises from your not using sufficient exercise," answered the King. "I use, nevertheless," said the Duke, "constant and severe exercise of every kind. But there is another effort requisite in order to repress this tendency which is much more difficult to practise, and without which no exercise, however violent, will suffice. I mean great renunciation and temperance. Nothing else can prevent your Majesty from growing to my size." The King made little reply, but the Duke's words sunk deep and produced a lasting impression on his mind. From that day he formed the resolution, as he assured Lord Mansfield, of checking his constitutional inclination to corpulency by unremitting restraint upon his appetite, a determination which he carried into complete effect in defiance of every temptation.

Perhaps no sovereign of whom history, ancient or modern, makes mention in any age of the earth has exceeded him in the practice of this virtue. It is a fact that during many years of his life, after coming up from Kew or from Windsor, often on horseback and sometimes in heavy rain, to the Queen's house, he has gone in a sedan-chair to St. James's, dressed himself, held a levée, passed through all the forms of that long and tedious ceremony, for such it was in the way that he performed it,

without leaving any individual in the circle unnoticed, and has afterwards assisted at a Privy Council, or given audience to his Cabinet Ministers and others, till five, and even sometimes till six o'clock. After so much fatigue of body and of mind, the only refreshment or sustenance that he usually took consisted of a few slices of bread and butter and a dish of tea, which he sometimes swallowed as he walked up and down, previous to getting into his carriage in order to return into the country. His understanding, solid and sedate, qualified him admirably for business, though it was neither of a brilliant, lively, nor imposing description. But his manner did injustice to the endowments of his intellect, and, unfortunately, it was in public that these minute personal defects or imperfections became most conspicuous. Dr. Johnson, indeed, thought otherwise on the subject; for, after the conversation with which his Majesty was pleased to honour that great literary character in the library of the Queen's house in February 1767, he passed the highest encomiums on the elegant manners of the sovereign. Boswell, in Johnson's Life, speaking of this circumstance, adds, "He said to Mr. Barnard, the librarian, 'Sir, they may talk of the King as they will, but he is the finest gentleman I have ever seen.' And he afterwards observed to Mr. Langton, 'Sir, his manners are those of as fine a gentleman as we may suppose Louis XIV or Charles II.'"

Independent of the effect necessarily produced on Johnson's mind by so unexpected and flattering a mark of royal condescension, which may well be imagined to have operated most favourably on the opinions of the moralist, he was perhaps of all men the least capable of estimating personal elegance of deportment. His vast intellectual powers lay in another line of discrimination. Had Johnson been now living, he might indeed witness the finest model of grace, dignity, ease, and affability which the world has ever beheld united in the same person. In *him* are really blended the majesty of Louis XIV with the amenity of Charles II.[1] But George III was altogether destitute of these ornamental and adventitious endowments. The oscillations of his body, the precipitation of his questions, none of which, it was said, would wait for an answer, and the hurry of his articulation afforded, on the contrary, to little minds or to malicious observers, who only saw him at the drawing-room (or, as the Duchess of Chandos called it, the *drawling* room), occasion for calling in question the soundness of his judgment and the strength of his faculties. None of his Ministers, however, and Mr. Fox, if possible, less than any other, entertained such an opinion. His whole reign forms, indeed, the best answer to the imputation. That he committed many errors, nourished many prejudices, formed many erroneous estimates, and frequently adhered too pertinaciously to his determinations, where he conceived, perhaps falsely, that they were founded in reason or in justice—all these allegations may be admitted. Nor can the injurious effects to himself and to his people, necessarily flowing in various instances from such defects of character and of administration, be altogether denied. But these infirmities, from which no man is exempt, cannot impugn his right to the affectionate veneration of posterity for the inflexible uprightness of his public conduct; and as little can they deprive him of the suffrages of the wise and good of every age, who will bear testimony to the expansion of his mind and the invariable rectitude of his intentions.

It would indeed be difficult for history to produce an instance of any prince who has united and displayed on the throne during near half a century so many personal and private virtues. In the flower of youth, unmarried, endowed with a vigorous constitution, and surrounded with temptations to pleasure or indulgence of every kind when

he succeeded to the crown, he never yielded to these seductions. Not less affectionately attached to the Queen than Charles I was to his consort Henrietta Maria, he remained, nevertheless, altogether exempt from the uxoriousness which characterised his unfortunate predecessor, and which operated so fatally in the course of his reign.

Wilkes, in the papers of the "North Briton," and "Junius," always affected, by drawing comparisons between the two kings, to demonstrate the moral resemblance that existed between them; but the pretended similarity was only external, in matters of mere deportment, not of solid character. It must be apparent to every impartial person who studies their respective reigns and lines of political action how superior was George III to Charles on the three great points that constitute the essential differences between men. The first of these qualities was firmness of mind. To his weakness, not even to give it a more severe epithet, in abandoning Lord Strafford to the rage of his enemies, we may trace all the misfortunes that accompanied Charles from that time down to the close of life, misfortunes aggravated by the reproaches of his own conscience for delivering up his Minister a victim to popular violence. His present Majesty neither deserted Lord Bute when most unpopular, in 1763, nor the Duke of Grafton amidst the tumults of March 1769, nor Lord North in the more awful riots of June 1780. As little did he turn his back on Lord George Germain after the defeats of Saratoga or of Yorktown, amidst the disasters of the American war. Far from recurring for support to his Ministers, he constantly extended it to them, and never shrank from personal risk, responsibility, or odium. His conduct on the memorable 7th of June 1780, both at the council table and during the course of that calamitous night which followed, will best exemplify the assertion. Charles, though personally brave in the field, and perfectly composed on the scaf-

[1] A compliment to the Prince Regent, eldest son of George III, who succeeded him as George IV in 1820.

fold, was deficient in political courage, steadiness of temper, and tenacity of determination. These qualities formed the distinguishing characteristics of George III, who seems, when assailed by misfortunes, to have taken as his motto the sentiment of the Roman poet—

"Tu ne cede malis; sed contra, audentior ito." [2]

Nor does the balance incline less in his favour when compared with his predecessor of the Stuart line in the article of judgment. If any act of his present Majesty's reign or government may seem to bear an analogy to the intemperate, vindictive, and pernicious attempt of Charles to seize on the five members of the House of Commons, it was the order issued by a general warrant to take Wilkes into custody. Nor shall I undertake the defence of that proceeding, which I have always considered as the least justifiable measure in every sense embraced since the King's accession to the throne. But when he authorised it in April 1763, he had not completed his twenty-fifth year. Charles I was above forty at the time of his committing the rash act in question. That George III, if he had ever been reduced to take up arms against his subjects, might, from the partialities of parental affection, have committed an error similar to that of Charles when he intrusted the command of his forces to Prince Rupert, I will even admit to be probable, reasoning from the internal evidence afforded by the campaigns of 1793, 1794, and 1799.[3] But no man who has followed the whole chain of events from 1760 down to 1810 can hesitate in pronouncing that under circumstances the most appalling to the human mind, demanding equal fortitude and intellectual

resources, he has displayed a degree of ability that we would vainly seek in the Stuart king's unfortunate administration, terminated by the scaffold.

It is, however, in moral principle and good faith that the superiority of the one sovereign over the other becomes most irresistible, and forces the completest conviction. "Charles I," says Junius, "lived and died a hypocrite." However severe we may esteem this sentence, we cannot contest that his insincerity formed a prominent feature of his character, and eminently conduced to his destruction. It was proved by a variety of facts, and it unquestionably deterred Cromwell, as well as others of the republican leaders, from exhibiting or anticipating the conduct of Monk. Unable to trust his most solemn assurances, they found no security for themselves except in bringing him to the block. But George III exhibited a model of unshaken fidelity to his engagements, even those most repugnant to his own feelings and most contrary to his own judgment. I could adduce many proofs of the fact. How magnanimous was his reception and treatment of Adams in 1783 — a man personally obnoxious — when presented to him at his levée as envoy from the American States! In terms the most conciliating, yet nobly frank, he avowed to that Minister with what reluctance he had consented to the separation of the Transatlantic British colonies from his dominion; "but," added he, "their independence being now consummated, I shall be the last man in my kingdom to encourage its violation."

* * *

After having thus faithfully portrayed, though in the seeming language of panegyric, the character of George III, it is impossible, nevertheless, without violating truth, to deny that at this time, far from being popular, he was not even an object of general affection. We may justly question whether Charles II, though one of the most unprincipled, profligate, and licen-

---

[2] "Do not yield to misfortunes; but instead go forth against them boldly." Vergil, *Aeneid*, V, 95.
[3] A reference to George III's appointment of his second son, Frederick Augustus, Duke of York, to command of the British army in Flanders, 1793–1795, and to commander-in-chief, 1798–1809.

tious sovereigns who ever reigned in this country, destitute of morals, sunk in dissolute pleasures, who tamely beheld his fleet burned by the Dutch in his own harbours, a pensioner of France, insensible to national glory, and regardless of the subjection of the Continent to Louis XIV, yet was ever so unpopular at any period of his reign. In order to explain this seeming paradox and to show how a prince who apparently from his many private virtues should have possessed the attachment of his subjects, was nevertheless considered by a very large proportion of them with contrary sentiments, we must review the principal features of his Government. That retrospect will fully account for the circumstance, while it elucidates the events which followed the commencement of the year 1781.

To the confined plan of education and sequestered life which the King led subsequent to the death of his father before his own accession to the crown may be justly traced and attributed, at least in part, many of the errors as well as the misfortunes that mark the portion of the British annals from 1760 down to the close of the American war. During near ten years which elapsed between the demise of Frederick, Prince of Wales, early in 1751, and the decease of George II, a period when the human mind is susceptible of such deep impressions, he remained in a state of almost absolute seclusion from his future people and from the world. Constantly resident at Leicester House or at Carlton House when he was in London; immured at Kew whenever he went to breathe the air of the country; perpetually under the eye of his mother and of Lord Bute, who acted in the closest unity of design, he saw comparatively few other persons, and those only chosen individuals of both sexes. They naturally obtained and long preserved a very firm ascendant over him. When he ascended the throne, though already arrived at manhood, his very person was hardly known, and his character was still less understood beyond a narrow circle. Precautions, it is

well ascertained, were even adopted by the Princess Dowager to preclude, as much as possible, access to him—precautions which, to the extent of her ability, were redoubled after he became king. It will scarcely be believed, but it is nevertheless true, that, in order to prevent his conversing with any persons or receiving any written intimations, anonymous or otherwise, between the drawing-room and the door of Carlton House, when he was returning from thence to St. James's Palace, or to Buckingham House after his evening visits to his mother, she never failed to accompany him till he got into his sedan-chair. "Junius," in May 1770, after invidiously comparing Edward II and Richard II (two of the weakest or most misguided princes who ever reigned in this country) with George III, adds, when summing up the leading features of his character, "Secluded from the world, attached from his infancy to one set of persons and one set of ideas, he can neither open his heart to new connections nor his mind to better information. A character of this sort is the soil fittest to produce that obstinate bigotry in politics and religion which begins with meritorious sacrifice of the understanding, and finally conducts the monarch and the martyr to the block."

A prince who had been endowed by nature with great energies of mind would, no doubt, have soon liberated himself from such fetters. Yet we may remember that Louis XIV, who, whatever faults he committed in the course of his long reign, must nevertheless always be considered as a sovereign of very superior intellectual endowments, remained under the tutelage of his mother and his Minister, of Anne of Austria and Cardinal Mazarin, till even a later period of life than twenty-two. Nor did he then emancipate himself. It was death that, by carrying off the Cardinal, allowed the King to display those qualities which have rendered so celebrated his name and reign. A prince, on the other hand, of a gay, social, dissipated, or convivial disposition would equally have burst through these impediments. But pleasure of every kind, in the common acceptation of the term, as meaning dissipation, presented scarcely any attractions for him even previous to his marriage. Stories were indeed generally circulated of his attachment to a young woman, a Quaker, about this time of his life, just as scandal many years afterwards whispered that he distinguished Lady Bridget Tollemache by his particular attentions. The former report was probably well founded, and the latter assertion was unquestionably true, but those persons who have enjoyed most opportunities for studying the King's character will most incline to believe that in neither instance did he pass the limits of innocent gallantry or occasional familiarity. As little was he to be seduced by the gratifications of the table, of wine, or of festivity. To all these allurements he seemed disinclined from natural constitution, moral and physical. His brother, Edward, Duke of York, plunged, on the contrary, very early into every sort of excess; but the example produced no effect on a prince modest, reserved, continent, capable of great self-command, and seeking almost all his amusements within a narrow domestic circle.

The Constitutional King

JOHN ADOLPHUS

John Adolphus (1768–1845) was a barrister whose principal interest was the writing of history. His historical apprenticeship was served under one of the great figures in eighteenth century historiography, Archdeacon William Coxe (1747–1828), and his own works followed the sober, thorough, carefully documented style of Coxe. Adolphus' works are temperate and judicious in tone, although marked by a conservative outlook and strong anti-Jacobin feeling. His major work is his *The History of England from the Accession to the Decease of King George the Third*, which, despite the title, he was able to bring only to the year 1804.

I HAVE never been able, nor has the course of my reading given me the inclination, to coincide with those authors or orators who are pleased to inveigh, with almost indiscriminate severity, against the foreign and domestic government of Great Britain. These highly seasoned invectives may be gratifying to some readers; and to them the more plain, tranquil narrative of undisguised fact may seem insipid: but reputation derived from such sources has never been the object of my desire; I confine myself, with strict forbearance, to the paths where I expect to find certain truth, and do not, in order to be thought courageous, attack where I am sure not to be encountered, nor calumniate those who by station, circumstances, time, or death, are rendered undesirous or incapable of resentment. Far from envying the applauses obtained by those disciples of Thersites, who claim the merit of wit and courage by rancorous abuse on the sovereign, government, and constitution of the country, I can with-

From John Adolphus, *The History of England from the Accession to the Decease of King George the Third*, 7 vols. (London, 1840), vol. I, pp, vi–vii, 1–5, 11–13, 335–337.

out hesitation declare my opinion, that, in the period on which I have written, the throne has been filled by a monarch who has sought the love of his subjects through the means of public spirit and private virtue; and who has tempered a noble desire to preserve from degradation the authority he inherits, with a firm and just regard to the constitution and liberties which conducted him to the throne, and which will ever form its best supports. Far from thinking that the aims of successive administrations have been directed to overthrow the liberties and constitution of the country, I am persuaded that liberty has been better understood, and more effectually and practically promoted during this period, than in any which preceded; and that the affairs of government have been always honestly, though sometimes imprudently, and in the conspicuous instance of the American war, unsuccessfully, administered.

*   *   *

George the Second was succeeded by his grandson, the son of Frederick Prince of Wales, and of Augusta Princess of Saxe Gotha, who had recently completed his twenty-second year.

Since the death of his father (20th March, 1751), the Heir Apparent had resided entirely with the Princess Dowager, who attended to his education with maternal solicitude. The party, which, during the life of Prince Frederick, had been considered as devoted to his interest, was, since his death, entirely dissolved. The Princess herself did not encourage any opposition to government; and the individuals, whom hope or affection attached to the late Prince, had retired from the field of politics, or formed new connexions.

Yet the education of a Prince, who was in time to govern a mighty kingdom, was not regarded with indifference by those whose interests might be affected by the ascendancy of rivals, or who feared that, if the Princess herself retained the influence which might be naturally expected,

new arrangements would be made, unfavourable to their views and adverse to their opinions.

Unfortunately, George II entertained a constant jealousy and suspicion of the Princess, which, long cherished, had grown into dislike, and made those who were desirous of his favour, carefully avoid all apparent intercourse with his daughter-in-law; consequently, the young Prince was wholly unacquainted with the sentiments and manners of those who formed his grandfather's court. This neglect extended even to the royal family; and the Duke of Cumberland and Princess Amelia shewed no marks of attention and respect to the Heir Apparent and his mother.

Encouraged by these circumstances, and actuated by views of ambition, Lord Harcourt, who had been appointed governor to the young Prince, and Dr. Hayter, Bishop of Norwich, who filled the post of preceptor, not only exerted their influence to detach his affections from all who had enjoyed the favour of his deceased parent, but also, by their example and discourse, imparted sentiments of disrespect toward the Princess Dowager; for which, at a subsequent period, the Prince acknowledged his error with honest contrition, and suitable apologies. In consequence of these efforts, divisions arose among those to whom the instruction of the Heir Apparent was confided, and a representation was made to the King, that Mr. Stone, subgovernor of His Royal Highness, was an improper person to be intrusted with his education; he was stated to be a Jacobite, and accused of having, in company with Dr. Johnson, Bishop of Gloucester, and Mr. Murray, the solicitor-general, afterward Earl of Mansfield, drunk the health of the Pretender and Lord Dunbar. The matter was referred by the King to the cabinet council. Fawcett was examined; but the charge was so frivolous, and the prevarications of Fawcett so gross and evident, the denials of Mr. Murray and Dr. Johnson so clear, precise, and satisfactory, that the lords unanimously represented to the King, that there was no foundation for any part of the charge.

Upon this decision, Lord Harcourt and the Bishop of Norwich declared their resolution to resign, unless Mr. Stone, Mr. Scott, sub-preceptor to the Prince, and Mr. Cresset, secretary to the Princess Dowager, were dismissed; for they, it was said, cherished Jacobite principles, and instilled arbitrary notions into the Prince. The King received this unfounded complaint with due indifference, the proffered resignations were accepted, and, not without some hesitation on his part, Lord Waldegrave was appointed governor; the Bishop of Peterborough was nominated preceptor.

To interest the public in this dispute, an anonymous letter was transmitted by the penny post to a popular preacher, advising him to notice in the pulpit the Prince's dangerous education; and to Lord Ravensworth, General Hawley, and a few other persons, purporting to be a representation or remonstrance from the Whig nobility and gentry, containing many injurious reflections on the education of the Prince, and the principles of his attendants. This paper was fabricated by Horace Walpole, afterward Earl of Oxford; the apparent motive for sending it was, a hope that it would be given to the Duke of Cumberland to lay before the King, and make impressions favourable to the views of the supposed writers.

The accusation against the Bishop of Gloucester, Mr. Murray, and Mr. Stone, was subsequently discussed in the House of Lords, on a motion for an address, praying His Majesty to submit to the House the whole proceeding before the privy council. The business was fully and freely investigated, as the King had granted to the members of the cabinet dispensations from the obligation of their oath as privy-counsellors; but, after a long and heavy debate, the House coincided in opinion with the council so entirely, that only three peers and one bishop offered to divide with the Duke of Bedford, who made the motion.

The public, whom this discussion was principally intended to alarm, easily discerned that the chief object was to remove the Pelham ministry, and to separate the Prince from the person and care of his parent; but all good men were satisfied that he should continue under her direction, and that she should preserve that influence over him which nature and policy equally declared to be her due.

From the satisfaction with which the Prince received the instructions of his new preceptor, the Bishop of Peterborough, sanguine hopes were entertained that he would derive much advantage from his tuition. To impart a knowledge of books was not the difficulty; in that particular no deficiency was complained of; but it was necessary to imbue the mind of the future sovereign with just notions of the British constitution and jurisprudence, and enable him to estimate correctly the national wealth and resources, and the means of preserving and increasing them. It was a great object of the Princess's care to educate her son in the principles and constant practice of religion; and with this view she invited the learned and pious Dr. Stephen Hales into her family, and appointed him clerk of the closet. Her good intentions were greatly favoured by the disposition of the Prince, who was affectionate, gentle, and exempt from every appearance of vicious inclination. The dread which the Princess constantly entertained, that his morals would be contaminated by the example of the young nobility, prevented his mixing with them in familiar intercourse, and his acquaintance was almost confined to the social circle of Leicester House; which was select, cheerful, and unrestrained.

On attaining his majority, the Prince took his seat in the House of Peers; but there was no debate in that session.

*   *   *

The King's friendship for the Earl of Bute led to extensive and permanent consequences. John Earl of Bute was son of

James second Earl of Bute, by Ann Campbell, daughter of Archibald first Duke of Argyle. He received his education at Eton; and at an early period of his life became a lord of the bedchamber of Frederick Prince of Wales. On the death of the Prince he retired, and took no share in political transactions, although often consulted by the Princess. On the establishment of the young Prince's household, he was appointed groom of the stole, and so continued after his accession. He had not occupied any public office; was unacquainted with the business and intrigues of state; and although he possessed an active mind, replete with elegant and abstruse learning, and was well acquainted with the theory of the British constitution, he was not competent to the task of instructing a future Sovereign in the practical science of governing a kingdom, where the component parts of the legislature were so nicely balanced, and their respective powers and operations so strictly guarded. It could not afford ground of surprise that the King, young and unacquainted with the persons of those who formed a successful and popular administration, should place among his confidential servants a nobleman whom he had long esteemed, and who possessed the confidence and good opinion of his parent: it could not be a subject of animadversion, that such a person should obtain a portion of the King's regard; nor would this circumstance have affected the course of political affairs, had not a new system followed his introduction into the cabinet.

The last two monarchs, being foreigners, and opposed by a native Prince who had numerous adherents, as well among the people as in some of the most illustrious houses, entrusted a large portion of their power to a few distinguished families, in order to secure possession of the crown. These families, strengthened by union and exclusive influence, became not only independent of, but in many respects superior to, the throne. Swayed by a predilection

for their continental dominions, the first two Sovereigns of the House of Hanover incurred severe animadversions from the members of opposition; and the necessity of frequent justifications rendering them still more dependent on the leaders of the ministerial party, reduced them almost to a state of pupilage.

But the new King, being exempt from foreign partialities, ascending the throne at a period when the claims of the exiled family were fallen into disregard, was enabled to emancipate himself from the restraint to which his predecessors had submitted. The Earl of Bute formed the plan of breaking the phalanx which constituted and supported the ministry, and of securing the independence of the crown, by a moderate exertion of constitutional prerogative. This plan in itself was well conceived, and necessary; but the Earl of Bute was not a proper person to carry it into effect. He was not connected, either by blood or by familiar intercourse, with the leading families in England; he was not versed in the arts of popularity, nor used to the struggles of parliamentary opposition; and his manners were cold, reserved, and unconciliating. He had not, as a measure preparatory to the assumption of power, secured an interest in either house of parliament, or among the people. Prejudices were easily excited against him as a native of Scotland; for it is to be recollected, that only fifteen years had elapsed since a rebellion begun in that country, had raged in the very heart of England, and he could only oppose to a popular and triumphant administration and a long established system, such friends as hope or interest might supply, and the personal esteem of the King, which was rendered less valuable by the odium attached to the name of favourite.

*   *   *

At the dissolution of the first parliament called by George III the aspect of affairs presented no consolatory views to his mind.[1] The King, from the beginning of his reign, had manifestly sought the advantage and honour of his people; yet such were the effects of a constant and acrimonious opposition, that not only the prudence of his measures, but the purity of his intentions was doubted. At his accession, he found a large portion of his subjects, conspicuous both for property and talent, excluded from all share in the government, and, by an affected stigma, rendered incapable of enjoying confidence, or rendering service to the crown. He relieved them from this proscription, and sought, by abolishing party and national distinctions, to reign King and protector of all his people. This measure, so wise and just in itself, was productive of endless feuds and jealousies. Every introduction of a new servant or family occasioned dissatisfaction and disgust: the disappointed formed new parties, avowed new principles, and sought by every device to distress and impede the operations of government. Thus so many successive ministries, who assumed the direction of public affairs, were all feeble and inefficient, while no single opposition was in itself strong or respectable. Every leader of a party commanded his share of influence, which, joined to that resulting from ministerial situation, was sufficient to procure a majority; but the parliament itself, delivered to so many opposite leaders, making laws in one session, repealing them in the next, affirming a principle at one period, and retracting it at another, lost much of the respect and confidence which ought to flow from the people to their representatives.

The King's benevolence was conspicuous in every act which he performed or sanctioned. He found the country at war: it was the first wish of his heart to restore the blessings of peace. In pursuit of this object he made no sacrifice of the national honour, but raised the glories of the country by a campaign of matchless vigour and success. From this circumstance resulted much of the obloquy thrown on the peace: the prosperous progress of the British arms inspired exaggerated hopes, and many who affected to deplore the miseries of war, decried the peace because it was not founded on principles which would have furnished an unanswerable motive for future aggression.

Against the private life of the King calumny itself could not discover an objection. Vice of every kind was not only unpractised, but discountenanced, at court; and it was not possible to survey, without an accumulated sense of respect and admiration, the first personage in the realm, although in the prime of youth, the most conspicuous in the performance of every social duty, and the most happy in the interesting centre of a domestic circle.

The King was a patron and liberal encourager of the polite arts, and anxious to give them a permanent establishment in Great Britain. At an early period of the reign, Lord Bute asserted, from his own knowledge, that rewards would never be wanting, provided proper subjects occurred, worthy of the royal protection; and the institution of the Royal Academy displayed at once the King's judgment, spirit, and patriotism.

Notwithstanding, however, his blameless life, and constant exertions to deserve the affection of his subjects, the King was not happy. The unceasing efforts of opposition in every part of his dominions, and the success which attended those insidious and baleful endeavours, deprived him of a great portion of tranquillity. His firmness, fortunately, prevented him from relinquishing a mode of conduct which his judgment led him to adopt; but although he was enabled to break the established phalanx, which, while it supported, obscured the throne, the struggle was attended with many painful circumstances.

[1] Reference is to the year 1768.

The King and the Cabal

EDMUND BURKE

Edmund Burke (1729–1797) left his native Ireland to pursue a literary career in London, but found his place in life as a politician and the principal spokesman of the Rockingham group in the House of Commons. After Rockingham's death in 1782 Burke continued to work with the group, now led by the Duke of Portland and Charles James Fox, until his dramatic break with Fox in 1791 on the question of the French Revolution. In 1770, in Burke's opinion, the principal danger to the English constitution lay in the growth of "the influence of the crown," and his *Thoughts on the Causes of the Present Discontents* expressed this fear. Later he saw a threat in the speculative reforming ideas of the French Revolution. Throughout his career, despite his strong partisanship and his tendency to exaggeration, ran the consistent thread of his dedication to the traditional institutions of England and his determination to preserve them for future generations.

THE power of the crown, almost dead and rotten as Prerogative, has grown up anew, with much more strength, and far less odium, under the name of Influence. An influence, which operated without noise and without violence; an influence, which converted the very antagonist into the instrument of power; which contained in itself a perpetual principle of growth and renovation; and which the distresses and the prosperity of the country equally tended to augment, was an admirable substitute for a prerogative, that, being only the offspring of antiquated prejudices, had moulded in its original stamina irresistible principles of decay and dissolution. The ignorance of the people is a bottom but for a temporary system; the interest of active men in the state is a foundation perpetual and infallible. However, some circumstances, arising, it must be confessed, in a great degree from accident, prevented the effects of this influence for a long time from breaking out in a manner capable of exciting any serious apprehensions. Although government was strong and flourished exceedingly, the *court* had drawn far less advantage than one would imagine from this great source of power.

At the Revolution, the crown, deprived, for the ends of the Revolution itself, of many prerogatives, was found too weak to struggle against all the difficulties which pressed so new and unsettled a government. The court was obliged therefore to delegate a part of its powers to men of such interest as could support, and of such fidelity as would adhere to, its establishment. Such men were able to draw in a greater number to a concurrence in the common defence. This connexion, necessary at first, continued long after convenient; and properly conducted might indeed, in all situations, be an useful instrument of government. At the same time, through the intervention of men of popular weight and character, the people possessed a security for their just proportion of importance

From Edmund Burke, *The Works of the Right Honourable Edmund Burke,* 6 vols. (London, 1871), vol. I, pp. 313–321, 324–331, 355–356, 369, 371, 379–381.

in the state. But as the title to the crown grew stronger by long possession, and by the constant increase of its influence, these helps have of late seemed to certain persons no better than encumbrances. The powerful managers for government were not sufficiently submissive to the pleasure of the possessors of immediate and personal favour, sometimes from a confidence in their own strength natural and acquired; sometimes from a fear of offending their friends, and weakening that lead in the country, which gave them a consideration independent of the court. Men acted as if the court could receive, as well as confer, an obligation. The influence of government, thus divided in appearance between the court and the leaders of parties, became in many cases an accession rather to the popular than to the royal scale; and some part of that influence, which would otherwise have been possessed as in a sort of mortmain and unalienable domain, returned again to the great ocean from whence it arose, and circulated among the people. This method, therefore, of governing by men of great natural interest or great acquired consideration, was viewed in a very invidious light by the true lovers of absolute monarchy. It is the nature of despotism to abhor power held by any means but its own momentary pleasure; and to annihilate all intermediate situations between boundless strength on its own part, and total debility on the part of the people.

To get rid of all this intermediate and independent importance, and *to secure to the court the unlimited and uncontrolled use of its own vast influence, under the sole direction of its own private favour*, has for some years past been the great object of policy. If this were compassed, the influence of the crown must of course produce all the effects which the most sanguine partisans of the court could possibly desire. Government might then be carried on without any concurrence on the part of the people; without any attention to the

dignity of the greater, or to the affections of the lower sorts. A new project was therefore devised by a certain set of intriguing men, totally different from the system of administration which had prevailed since the accession of the House of Brunswick. This project, I have heard, was first conceived by some persons in the court of Frederic Prince of Wales.

The earliest attempt in the execution of this design was to set up for minister, a person, in rank indeed respectable, and very ample in fortune; but who, to the moment of this vast and sudden elevation, was little known or considered in the kingdom. To him the whole nation was to yield an immediate and implicit submission. But whether it was from want of firmness to bear up against the first opposition; or that things were not yet fully ripened, or that this method was not found the most eligible; that idea was soon abandoned. The instrumental part of the project was a little altered, to accommodate it to the time, and to bring things more gradually and more surely to the one great end proposed.

The first part of the reformed plan was to draw *a line which should separate the court from the ministry*. Hitherto these names had been looked upon as synonymous; but for the future, court and administration were to be considered as things totally distinct. By this operation, two systems of administration were to be formed; one which should be in the real secret and confidence; the other merely ostensible to perform the official and executory duties of government. The latter were alone to be responsible; whilst the real advisers, who enjoyed all the power, were effectually removed from all the danger.

Secondly, *A party under these leaders was to be formed in favour of the court against the ministry*: this party was to have a large share in the emoluments of government, and to hold it totally separate from, and independent of, ostensible administration.

The third point, and that on which the success of the whole scheme ultimately depended, was *to bring parliament to an acquiescence in this project*. Parliament was therefore to be taught by degrees a total indifference to the persons, rank, influence, abilities, connexions, and character of the ministers of the crown. By means of a discipline, on which I shall say more hereafter, that body was to be habituated to the most opposite interests, and the most discordant politics. All connexions and dependencies among subjects were to be entirely dissolved. As, hitherto, business had gone through the hands of leaders of Whigs or Tories, men of talents to conciliate the people, and to engage their confidence; now the method was to be altered; and the lead was to be given to men of no sort of consideration or credit in the country. This want of natural importance was to be their very title to delegated power. Members of parliament were to be hardened into an insensibility to pride as well as to duty. Those high and haughty sentiments, which are the great support of independence, were to be let down gradually. Points of honour and precedence were no more to be regarded in parliamentary decorum, than in a Turkish army. It was to be avowed, as a constitutional maxim, that the king might appoint one of his footmen, or one of your footmen, for minister; and that he ought to be, and that he would be, well followed as the first name for rank or wisdom in the nation. Thus parliament was to look on, as if perfectly unconcerned, while a cabal of the closet and back-stairs was substituted in the place of a national administration.

With such a degree of acquiescence, any measure of any court might well be deemed thoroughly secure. The capital objects, and by much the most flattering characteristics, of arbitrary power, would be obtained. Everything would be drawn from its holdings in the country to the personal favour and inclination of the prince. This favour would be the sole introduction to power, and the only tenure by which it

was to be held: so that no person looking towards another, and all looking towards the court, it was impossible but that the motive which solely influenced every man's hopes must come in time to govern every man's conduct; till at last the servility became universal, in spite of the dead letter of any laws or institutions whatsoever.

How it should happen that any man could be tempted to venture upon such a project of government, may at first view appear surprising. But the fact is, that opportunities very inviting to such an attempt have offered; and the scheme itself was not destitute of some arguments, not wholly unplausible, to recommend it. These opportunities and these arguments, the use that has been made of both, the plan for carrying this new scheme of government into execution, and the effects which it has produced, are in my opinion worthy of our serious consideration.

His Majesty came to the throne of these kingdoms with more advantages than any of his predecessors since the Revolution. Fourth in descent, and third in succession of his royal family, even the zealots of hereditary right, in him, saw something to flatter their favourite prejudices; and to justify a transfer of their attachments, without a change in their principles. The person and cause of the Pretender were become contemptible; his title disowned throughout Europe; his party disbanded in England. His Majesty came indeed to the inheritance of a mighty war; but, victorious in every part of the globe, peace was always in his power, not to negotiate, but to dictate. No foreign habitudes or attachments withdrew him from the cultivation of his power at home. His revenue for the civil establishment, fixed (as it was then thought) at a large, but definite sum, was ample without being invidious. His influence, by additions from conquest, by an augmentation of debt, by an increase of military and naval establishment, much strengthened and extended. And coming to the throne in the prime and full vigour of youth, as from affection there was a strong dislike, so from dread there seemed to be a general averseness, from giving anything like offence to a monarch, against whose resentment opposition could not look for a refuge in any sort of reversionary hope.

These singular advantages inspired his Majesty only with a more ardent desire to preserve unimpaired the spirit of that national freedom to which he owed a situation so full of glory. But to others it suggested sentiments of a very different nature. They thought they now beheld an opportunity (by a certain sort of statesmen never long undiscovered or employed) of drawing to themselves, by the aggrandizement of a court faction, a degree of power which they could never hope to derive from natural influence or from honourable service; and which it was impossible they could hold with the least security, whilst the system of administration rested upon its former bottom. In order to facilitate the execution of their design, it was necessary to make many alterations in political arrangement, and a signal change in the opinions, habits, and connexions of the greatest part of those who at that time acted in public.

In the first place, they proceeded gradually, but not slowly, to destroy everything of strength which did not derive its principal nourishment from the immediate pleasure of the court. The greatest weight of popular opinion and party connexion were then with the Duke of Newcastle and Mr. Pitt. Neither of these held their importance by the *new tenure* of the court; they were not therefore thought to be so proper as others for the services which were required by that tenure. It happened very favourably for the new system, that under a forced coalition there rankled an incurable alienation and disgust between the parties which composed the administration. Mr. Pitt was first attacked. Not satisfied with removing him from power, they endeavoured by various artifices to ruin his character. The other party seemed rather pleased to get rid of so oppressive a

support; not perceiving that their own fall was prepared by his, and involved in it. Many other reasons prevented them from daring to look their true situation in the face. To the great Whig families it was extremely disagreeable, and seemed almost unnatural, to oppose the administration of a prince of the House of Brunswick. Day after day they hesitated, and doubted, and lingered, expecting that other counsels would take place; and were slow to be persuaded, that all which had been done by the cabal was the effect not of humour, but of system. It was more strongly and evidently the interest of the new court faction, to get rid of the great Whig connexions, than to destroy Mr. Pitt. The power of that gentleman was vast indeed and merited; but it was in a great degree personal, and therefore transient. Theirs was rooted in the country. For, with a good deal less of popularity, they possessed a far more natural and fixed influence. Long possession of government; vast property; obligations of favours given and received; connexion of office; ties of blood, of alliance, of friendship; (things at that time supposed of some force;) the name of Whig, dear to the majority of the people; the zeal early begun and steadily continued to the royal family: all these together formed a body of power in the nation, which was criminal and devoted. The great ruling principle of the cabal, and that which animated and harmonized all their proceedings, how various soever they may have been, was to signify to the world, that the court would proceed upon its own proper forces only; and that the pretence of bringing any other into its service was an affront to it, and not a support. Therefore when the chiefs were removed, in order to go to the root, the whole party was put under a proscription, so general and severe as to take their hard-earned bread from the lowest officers, in a manner which had never been known before, even in general revolutions. But it was thought necessary effectually to destroy all dependencies but one; and to show an example of the firmness and rigour with which the new system was to be supported.

Thus for the time were pulled down, in the persons of the Whig leaders and of Mr. Pitt, (in spite of the services of the one at the accession of the royal family, and the recent services of the other in the war,) the *two only securities for the importance of the people; power arising from popularity; and power arising from connexion.* Here and there indeed a few individuals were left standing, who gave security for their total estrangement from the odious principles of party connexion and personal attachment; and it must be confessed that most of them have religiously kept their faith. Such a change could not however be made without a mighty shock to government.

To reconcile the minds of the people to all these movements, principles correspondent to them had been preached up with great zeal. Every one must remember that the cabal set out with the most astonishing prudery, both moral and political. Those, who in a few months after soused over head and ears into the deepest and dirtiest pits of corruption, cried out violently against the indirect practices in the electing and managing of parliaments, which had formerly prevailed. This marvellous abhorrence which the court had suddenly taken to all influence, was not only circulated in conversation through the kingdom, but pompously announced to the public, with many other extraordinary things, in a pamphlet which had all the appearance of a manifesto preparatory to some considerable enterprise. Throughout it was a satire, though in terms managed and decent enough, on the politics of the former reign. It was indeed written with no small art and address.

In this piece appeared the first dawning of the new system; there first appeared the idea (then only in speculation) of *separating the court from the administration;* of carrying everything from national connexion to personal regards; and of forming a regular party for that purpose, under the name of *king's men.*

To recommend this system to the people, a perspective view of the court, gorgeously painted, and finely illuminated from within, was exhibited to the gaping multitude. Party was to be totally done away, with all its evil works. Corruption was to be cast down from court, as *Atè* was from heaven. Power was thenceforward to be the chosen residence of public spirit; and no one was to be supposed under any sinister influence, except those who had the misfortune to be in disgrace at court, which was to stand in lieu of all vices and all corruptions. A scheme of perfection to be realized in a monarchy far beyond the visionary republic of Plato. The whole scenery was exactly disposed to captivate those good souls, whose credulous morality is so invaluable a treasure to crafty politicians. Indeed there was wherewithal to charm everybody, except those few who are not much pleased with professions of supernatural virtue, who know of what stuff such professions are made, for what purposes they are designed, and in what they are sure constantly to end. Many innocent gentlemen, who had been talking prose all their lives without knowing anything of the matter, began at last to open their eyes upon their own merits, and to attribute their not having been lords of the treasury and lords of trade many years before, merely to the prevalence of party, and to the ministerial power, which had frustrated the good intentions of the court in favour of their abilities. Now was the time to unlock the sealed fountain of royal bounty, which had been infamously monopolized and huckstered, and to let it flow at large upon the whole people. The time was come, to restore royalty to its original splendour. *Mettre le Roy hors de page,* became a sort of watchword. And it was constantly in the mouths of all the runners of the court, that nothing could preserve the balance of the constitution from being overturned by the rabble, or by a faction of the nobility, but to free the sovereign effectually from that ministerial tyranny under which the royal dignity had been oppressed in the person of his Majesty's grandfather.

These were some of the many artifices used to reconcile the people to the great change which was made in the persons who composed the ministry, and the still greater which was made and avowed in its constitution. As to individuals, other methods were employed with them; in order so thoroughly to disunite every party, and even every family, that *no concert, order, or effect, might appear in any future opposition.* And in this manner an administration without connexion with the people, or with one another, was first put in possession of government.

*   *   *

It must be remembered, that since the Revolution, until the period we are speaking of, the influence of the crown had been always employed in supporting the ministers of state, and in carrying on the public business according to their opinions. But the party now in question is formed upon a very different idea. It is to intercept the favour, protection, and confidence of the crown in the passage to its ministers; it is to come between them and their importance in parliament; it is to separate them from all their natural and acquired dependencies; it is intended as the control, not the support, of administration. The machinery of this system is perplexed in its movements, and false in its principle. It is formed on a supposition that the king is something external to his government; and that he may be honoured and aggrandized, even by its debility and disgrace. The plan proceeds expressly on the idea of enfeebling the regular executory power. It proceeds on the idea of weakening the state in order to strengthen the court. The scheme depending entirely on distrust, on disconnexion, on mutability by principle, on systematic weakness in every particular

member; it is impossible that the total result should be substantial strength of any kind.

As a foundation of their scheme, the cabal have established a sort of *rota* in the court. All sorts of parties, by this means, have been brought into administration; from whence few have had the good fortune to escape without disgrace; none at all without considerable losses. In the beginning of each arrangement no professions of confidence and support are wanting, to induce the leading men to engage. But while the ministers of the day appear in all the pomp and pride of power, while they have all their canvass spread out to the wind, and every sail filled with the fair and prosperous gale of royal favour, in a short time they find, they know not how, a current, which sets directly against them; which prevents all progress; and even drives them backwards. They grow ashamed and mortified in a situation, which, by its vicinity to power, only serves to remind them the more strongly of their insignificance. They are obliged either to execute the orders of their inferiors, or to see themselves opposed by the natural instruments of their office. With the loss of their dignity they lose their temper. In their turn they grow troublesome to that cabal which, whether it supports or opposes, equally disgraces and equally betrays them. It is soon found necessary to get rid of the heads of administration; but it is of their heads only. As there always are many rotten members belonging to the best connexions, it is not hard to persuade several to continue in office without their leaders. By this means the party goes out much thinner than it came in; and is only reduced in strength by its temporary possession of power. Besides, if by accident, or in course of changes, that power should be recovered, the junto have thrown up a retrenchment of these carcases, which may serve to cover themselves in a day of danger. They conclude, not unwisely, that such rotten members will become the first objects of disgust and resentment to their ancient connexions.

They contrive to form in the outward administration two parties at the least; which, whilst they are tearing one another to pieces, are both competitors for the favour and protection of the cabal; and, by their emulation, contribute to throw everything more and more into the hands of the interior managers.

A minister of state will sometimes keep himself totally estranged from all his colleagues; will differ from them in their councils, will privately traverse, and publicly oppose, their measures. He will, however, continue in his employment. Instead of suffering any mark of displeasure, he will be distinguished by an unbounded profusion of court rewards and caresses; because he does what is expected, and all that is expected, from men in office. He helps to keep some form of administration in being, and keeps it at the same time as weak and divided as possible.

However, we must take care not to be mistaken, or to imagine that such persons have any weight in their opposition. When, by them, administration is convinced of its insignificancy, they are soon to be convinced of their own. They never are suffered to succeed in their opposition. They and the world are to be satisfied, that neither office, nor authority, nor property, nor ability, eloquence, counsel, skill, or union, are of the least importance; but that the mere influence of the court, naked of all support, and destitute of all management, is abundantly sufficient for all its own purposes.

When any adverse connexion is to be destroyed, the cabal seldom appear in the work themselves. They find out some person of whom the party entertains a high opinion. Such a person they endeavour to delude with various pretences. They teach him first to distrust, and then to quarrel with, his friends; among whom, by the same arts, they excite a similar diffidence of him; so that in this mutual fear and distrust, he may suffer himself to be employed as the instrument in the change which is brought about. Afterwards they are sure to destroy him in his turn, by setting up in his place some person in whom he had himself reposed the greatest confidence, and who serves to carry off a considerable part of his adherents.

When such a person has broke in this manner with his connexions, he is soon compelled to commit some flagrant act of iniquitous, personal hostility against some of them, (such as an attempt to strip a particular friend of his family estate,) by which the cabal hope to render the parties utterly irreconcilable. In truth, they have so contrived matters, that people have a greater hatred to the subordinate instruments than to the principal movers.

As in destroying their enemies they make use of instruments not immediately belonging to their corps, so in advancing their own friends they pursue exactly the same method. To promote any of them to considerable rank or emolument, they commonly take care that the recommendation shall pass through the hands of the ostensible ministry: such a recommendation might however appear to the world, as some proof of the credit of ministers, and some means of increasing their strength. To prevent this, the persons so advanced are directed in all companies, industriously to declare that they are under no obligations whatsoever to administration; that they have received their office from another quarter; that they are totally free and independent.

When the faction has any job of lucre to obtain, or of vengeance to perpetrate, their way is, to select, for the execution, those very persons to whose habits, friendships, principles, and declarations, such proceedings are publicly known to be the most adverse; at once to render the instruments the more odious, and therefore the more dependent, and to prevent the people from ever reposing a confidence in any appearance of private friendship or public principle.

If the administration seem now and then, from remissness, or from fear of making themselves disagreeable, to suffer any popular excesses to go unpunished, the cabal immediately sets up some creature of theirs to raise a clamour against the ministers, as having shamefully betrayed the dignity of government. Then they compel the ministry to become active in conferring rewards and honours on the persons who have been the instruments of their disgrace; and, after having first vilified them with the higher orders for suffering the laws to sleep over the licentiousness of the populace, they drive them (in order to make amends for their former inactivity) to some act of atrocious violence, which renders them completely abhorred by the people. They who remember the riots which attended the Middlesex election, the opening of the present parliament, and the transactions relative to Saint George's Fields, will not be at a loss for an application of these remarks.

That this body may be enabled to compass all the ends of its institution, its members are scarcely ever to aim at the high and responsible offices of the state. They are distributed with art and judgment through all the secondary, but efficient, departments of office, and through the households of all the branches of the royal family: so as on one hand to occupy all the avenues to the throne; and on the other to forward or frustrate the execution of any measure, according to their own interests. For with the credit and support which they are known to have, though for the greater part in places which are only a genteel excuse for salary, they possess all the influence of the highest posts; and they dictate publicly in almost everything, even with a parade of superiority. Whenever they dissent (as it often happens) from their nominal leaders, the trained part of the senate, instinctively in the secret, is sure to follow them; provided the leaders, sensible of their situation, do not of themselves recede in time from their most declared opinions. This latter is generally the case. It will not be conceivable to any one who has not seen it, what pleasure is taken by the cabal in rendering these heads of office

thoroughly contemptible and ridiculous. And when they are become so, they have then the best chance for being well supported.

The members of the court faction are fully indemnified for not holding places on the slippery heights of the kingdom, not only by the lead in all affairs, but also by the perfect security in which they enjoy less conspicuous, but very advantageous, situations. Their places are in express legal tenure, or, in effect, all of them for life. Whilst the first and most respectable persons in the kingdom are tossed about like tennis balls, the sport of a blind and insolent caprice, no minister dares even to cast an oblique glance at the lowest of their body. If an attempt be made upon one of this corps, immediately he flies to sanctuary, and pretends to the most inviolable of all promises. No conveniency of public arrangement is available to remove any one of them from the specific situation he holds; and the slightest attempt upon one of them, by the most powerful minister, is a certain preliminary to his own destruction.

Conscious of their independence, they bear themselves with a lofty air to the exterior ministers. Like Janissaries, they derive a kind of freedom from the very condition of their servitude. They may act just as they please, provided they are true to the great ruling principle of their institution. It is, therefore, not at all wonderful, that people should be so desirous of adding themselves to that body, in which they may possess and reconcile satisfactions the most alluring, and seemingly the most contradictory; enjoying at once all the spirited pleasure of independence, and all the gross lucre and fat emoluments of servitude.

Here is a sketch, though a slight one, of the constitution, laws, and policy of this new court corporation. The name by which they choose to distinguish themselves, is that of *king's men,* or the *king's friends,* by an invidious exclusion of the rest of his Majesty's most loyal and affectionate subjects. The whole system, com-

prehending the exterior and interior administrations, is commonly called, in the
technical language of the court, *double
cabinet;* in French or English, as you
choose to pronounce it.

Whether all this be a vision of a distracted brain, or the invention of a malicious heart, or a real faction in the country,
must be judged by the appearances which
things have worn for eight years past. Thus
far I am certain, that there is not a single
public man, in or out of office, who has
not, at some time or other, borne testimony
to the truth of what I have now related.
In particular, no persons have been more
strong in their assertions, and louder and
more indecent in their complaints, than
those who compose all the exterior part of
the present administration; in whose time
that faction has arrived at such an height
of power, and of boldness in the use of it,
as may, in the end, perhaps bring about its
total destruction.

It is true, that about four years ago, during the administration of the Marquis of
Rockingham, an attempt was made to carry
on government without their concurrence.
However, this was only a transient cloud;
they were hid but for a moment; and their
constellation blazed out with greater bright-
ness, and a far more vigorous influence,
some time after it was blown over. An attempt was at that time made (but without
any idea of proscription) to break their
corps, to discountenance their doctrines, to
revive connexions of a different kind, to
restore the principles and policy of the
Whigs, to reanimate the cause of liberty by
ministerial countenance; and then for the
first time were men seen attached in office
to every principle they had maintained in
opposition. No one will doubt, that such
men were abhorred and violently opposed
by the court faction, and that such a system could have but a short duration.

It may appear somewhat affected, that in
so much discourse upon this extraordinary
party, I should say so little of the Earl of
Bute, who is the supposed head of it. But
this was neither owing to affectation nor

inadvertence. I have carefully avoided the
introduction of personal reflections of any
kind. Much the greater part of the topics
which have been used to blacken this
nobleman are either unjust or frivolous. At
best, they have a tendency to give the resentment of this bitter calamity a wrong
direction, and to turn a public grievance
into a mean, personal, or a dangerous national quarrel. Where there is a regular
scheme of operations carried on, it is the
system, and not any individual person who
acts in it, that is truly dangerous. This
system has not arisen solely from the ambition of Lord Bute, but from the circumstances which favoured it, and from an indifference to the constitution which had
been for some time growing among our
gentry. We should have been tried with it,
if the Earl of Bute had never existed; and it
will want neither a contriving head nor
active members, when the Earl of Bute
exists no longer. It is not, therefore, to rail
at Lord Bute, but firmly to embody against
this court party and its practices, which can
afford us any prospect of relief in our present condition.

Another motive induces me to put the
personal consideration of Lord Bute wholly
out of the question. He communicates very
little in a direct manner with the greater
part of our men of business. This has never
been his custom. It is enough for him that
he surrounds them with his creatures. Several imagine, therefore, that they have a
very good excuse for doing all the work of
this faction, when they have no personal
connexion with Lord Bute. But whoever
becomes a party to an administration, composed of insulated individuals, without faith
plighted, tie, or common principle; an administration constitutionally impotent, because supported by no party in the nation;
he who contributes to destroy the connexions of men and their trust in one another,
or in any sort to throw the dependence of
public counsels upon private will and favour, possibly may have nothing to do with
the Earl of Bute. It matters little whether
he be the friend or the enemy of that par-

ticular person. But let him be who or what he will, he abets a faction that is driving hard to the ruin of his country. He is sapping the foundation of its liberty, disturbing the sources of its domestic tranquillity, weakening its government over its dependencies, degrading it from all its importance in the system of Europe.

It is this unnatural infusion of a *system of favouritism* into a government which in a great part of its constitution is popular, that has raised the present ferment in the nation. The people, without entering deeply into its principles, could plainly perceive its effects, in much violence, in a great spirit of innovation, and a general disorder in all the functions of government. I keep my eye solely on this system; if I speak of those measures which have arisen from it, it will be so far only as they illustrate the general scheme. This is the fountain of all those bitter waters, of which, through an hundred different conduits, we have drunk until we are ready to burst. The discretionary power of the crown in the formation of ministry, abused by bad or weak men, has given rise to a system, which without directly violating the letter of any law, operates against the spirit of the whole constitution.

*   *   *

It behoves the people of England to consider how the House of Commons, under the operation of these examples, must of necessity be constituted. On the side of the court will be, all honours, offices, emoluments; every sort of personal gratification to avarice or vanity; and, what is of more moment to most gentlemen, the means of growing, by innumerable petty services to individuals, into a spreading interest in their country. On the other hand, let us suppose a person unconnected with the court, and in opposition to its system. For his own person, no office, or emolument, or title; no promotion ecclesiastical, or civil, or military, or naval, for children, or brothers, or kindred. In vain an expiring interest in a borough calls for offices, or small livings,

for the children of mayors, and aldermen, and capital burgesses. His court rival has them all. He can do an infinite number of acts of generosity and kindness, and even of public spirit. He can procure indemnity from quarters. He can procure advantages in trade. He can get pardons for offences. He can obtain a thousand favours, and avert a thousand evils. He may, while he betrays every valuable interest of the kingdom, be a benefactor, a patron, a father, a guardian angel, to his borough. The unfortunate independent member has nothing to offer, but harsh refusal, or pitiful excuse, or despondent representation of a hopeless interest. Except from his private fortune, in which he may be equalled, perhaps exceeded, by his court competitor, he has no way of showing any one good quality, or of making a single friend. In the House, he votes for ever in a dispirited minority. If he speaks, the doors are locked. A body of loquacious placemen go out to tell the world that all he aims at is to get into office. If he has not the talent of elocution, which is the case of many as wise and knowing men as any in the House, he is liable to all these inconveniencies, without the éclat which attends upon any tolerably successful exertion of eloquence. Can we conceive a more discouraging post of duty than this? Strip it of the poor reward of popularity; suffer even the excesses committed in defence of the popular interest to become a ground for the majority of that House to form a disqualification out of the line of the law, and at their pleasure, attended not only with the loss of the franchise, but with every kind of personal disgrace. — If this shall happen, the people of this kingdom may be assured that they cannot be firmly or faithfully served by any man.

*   *   *

Indeed, in the situation in which we stand, with an immense revenue, an enormous debt, mighty establishments, government itself a great banker and a great merchant, I see no other way for the preservation of a decent attention to public interest in the representatives, but *the interposition of the body of the people itself,* whenever it shall appear, by some flagrant and notorious act, by some capital innovation, that these representatives are going to over-leap the fences of the law, and to introduce an arbitrary power. This interposition is a most unpleasant remedy. But, if it be a legal remedy, it is intended on some occasion to be used; to be used then only, when it is evident that nothing else can hold the constitution to its true principles.

The distempers of monarchy were the great subjects of apprehension and redress, in the last century; in this, the distempers of parliament. It is not in parliament alone that the remedy for parliamentary disorders can be completed; hardly indeed can it begin there. Until a confidence in government is re-established, the people ought to be excited to a more strict and detailed attention to the conduct of their representatives. Standards for judging more systematically upon their conduct ought to be settled in the meetings of counties and corporations. Frequent and correct lists of the voters in all important questions ought to be procured.

By such means something may be done. By such means it may appear who those are, that, by an indiscriminate support of all administrations, have totally banished all integrity and confidence out of public proceedings; have confounded the best men with the worst; and weakened and dissolved, instead of strengthening and compacting, the general frame of government. If any person is more concerned for government and order, than for the liberties of his country, even he is equally concerned to put an end to this course of indiscriminate support. It is this blind and undistinguishing support, that feeds the spring of those very disorders, by which he is frightened into the arms of the faction which contains in itself the source of all disorders, by enfeebling all the visible and regular authority of the state.

*   *   *

Government may in a great measure be restored, if any considerable bodies of men have honesty and resolution enough never to accept administration, unless this garrison of *king's men,* which is stationed, as in a citadel, to control and enslave it, be entirely broken and disbanded, and every work they have thrown up be levelled with the ground. The disposition of public men to keep this corps together, and to act under it, or to co-operate with it, is a touch-stone by which every administration ought in future to be tried. There has not been one which has not sufficiently experienced the utter incompatibility of that faction with the public peace, and with all the ends of good government: since, if they opposed it, they soon lost every power of serving the crown; if they submitted to it, they lost all the esteem of their country. Until ministers give to the public a full proof of their entire alienation from that system, however plausible their pretences, we may be sure they are more intent on the emoluments than the duties of office. If they refuse to give this proof, we know of what stuff they are made. In this particular, it ought to be the electors' business to look to their representatives. The electors ought to esteem it no less culpable in their member to give a single vote in parliament to such an administration, than to take an office under it; to endure it, than to act in it. The notorious infidelity and versatility of members of parliament, in their opinions of men and things, ought in a particular manner to be considered by the electors in the inquiry which is recommended to them. This is one of the principal holdings of that destructive system, which has endeavoured to unhinge all the virtuous, honourable, and useful connexions in the kingdom.

*   *   *

If the reader believes that there really exists such a faction as I have described; a faction ruling by the private inclinations of a court, against the general sense of the people; and that this faction, whilst it pursues a scheme for undermining all the foundations of our freedom, weakens (for the present at least) all the powers of executory government, rendering us abroad contemptible, and at home distracted; he will believe also, that nothing but a firm combination of public men against this body, and that, too, supported by the hearty concurrence of the people at large, can possibly get the better of it. The people will see the necessity of restoring public men to an attention to the public opinion, and of restoring the constitution to its original principles. Above all, they will endeavour to keep the House of Commons from assuming a character which does not belong to it. They will endeavour to keep that House, for its existence, for its powers, and its privileges, as independent of every other, and as dependent upon themselves, as possible. This servitude is to a House of Commons (like obedience to the Divine law) "perfect freedom." For if they once quit this natural, rational, and liberal obedience, having deserted the only proper foundation of their power, they must seek a support in an abject and unnatural dependence somewhere else. When, through the medium of this just connexion with their constituents, the genuine dignity of the House of Commons is restored, it will begin to think of casting from it, with scorn, as badges of servility, all the false ornaments of illegal power, with which it has been, for some time, disgraced. It will begin to think of its old office of CONTROL.

It will not suffer that last of evils to predominate in the country; men without popular confidence, public opinion, natural connexion, or mutual trust, invested with all the powers of government.

When they have learned this lesson themselves, they will be willing and able to teach the court, that it is the true interest of the prince to have but one administration; and that one composed of those who recommend themselves to their sovereign through the opinion of their country, and not by their obsequiousness to a favourite. Such men will serve their sovereign with affection and fidelity; because his choice of them, upon such principles, is a compliment to their virtue. They will be able to serve him effectually; because they will add the weight of the country to the force of the executory power. They will be able to serve their king with dignity; because they will never abuse his name to the gratification of their private spleen or avarice. This, with allowances for human frailty, may probably be the general character of a ministry, which thinks itself accountable to the House of Commons, when the House of Commons thinks itself accountable to its constituents. If other ideas should prevail, things must remain in their present confusion; until they are hurried into all the rage of civil violence; or until they sink into the dead repose of despotism.

High Prerogative and the Freedom of the Subject

HORACE WALPOLE

Horace Walpole (1717–1797) was the fourth son of Sir Robert Walpole. He sat in Parliament from 1741 to 1768, but, despite his distinguished name, he did not rise to positions of leadership or responsibility. He was, in some respects, a shallow and vindictive man, filled with anxieties and resentments, all of which are displayed in his *Memoirs of the Reign of King George the Third*. This work combines hostility to the court with contempt for the principal opposition groups, and Walpole invariably finds a discreditable motive for any act. Despite these faults, Walpole's memoirs have genuine merits. Walpole was an inveterate seeker of "inside information," and he had an insatiable desire to record what he thought and heard. Walpole's memoirs, despite obvious prejudices and special pleading, remain an important source of information for students of the reign of George III.

No British monarch has ascended the throne with so many advantages as George the Third. Being the first of his line born in England, the prejudice against his family as foreigners ceased in his person — Hanover was no longer the native soil of our Princes; consequently, attachment to the Electorate was not likely to govern our councils, as it had done in the last two reigns. This circumstance, too, of his birth, shifted the unpopularity of foreign extraction from the House of Brunswick to the Stuarts. In the flower and bloom of youth, George had a handsome, open, and honest countenance; and with the favour that attends the outward accomplishments of his age, he had none of the vices that fall under the censure of those who are past enjoying them themselves.

The moment of his accession was fortunate beyond example. The extinction of parties had not waited for, but preceded, the dawn of his reign. Thus it was not a race of factions running to offer themselves, as is common, to a new Prince, bidding for his favour, and ready each to be disgusted if their antagonists were received with more grace; but a natural devolution of duty from all men to the uncontroverted heir of the Crown, who had no occasion to court the love of his subjects, nor could fear interrupting established harmony but by making any change in a system so well compacted. The administration was firm, in good harmony with one another, and headed by the most successful genius that ever presided over our councils. Conquests had crowned our arms with wonderful circumstances of glory and fortune; and the young King seemed to have the option of extending our victories and acquisitions, or of giving peace to the world, by finding himself in a situation so favourable, that neither his ambition nor moderation could have been equitably reprehended. The designs and offences of France would have justified a fuller measure of revenge; moderation could want no excuse.

A passionate, domineering woman, and a

From Horace Walpole, *Memoirs of the Reign of King George the Third,* ed. G. F. Russell Barker, 4 vols. (London, 1894), vol. I, pp. 3–4, 14–17, 82–83, 90–91, 95–96, 84.

Favourite, without talents, soon drew a cloud over this shining prospect.

* * *

The views of the Court were so fully manifested afterwards, that no doubt can be entertained but a plan had been early formed of carrying the prerogative to very unusual heights. The Princess was ardently fond of power, and all its appanages of observance, rank, and wealth. The deepest secrecy and dissimulation guarded every avenue of her passions; and close retirement was adapted to these purposes. She could not appear in public (after the arrival of the Queen) as the first woman of the kingdom: her unpopularity made her pride tremble; and privacy shrouded such hours as were not calculated to draw esteem; and it contracted her expenses. After the King's marriage she appeared seldom or never at St. James's, nor deigned to accompany the ceremony of the coronation. The attendance of her ladies was dispensed with except on drawing-room days; and by degrees even her maids of honour and women of the bedchamber were removed from her palace, where she lived in a solitude that would have passed for the perfection of Christian humility in the ages of monkish ignorance. Jealousy of her credit over her son made her impose almost as strict laws of retirement on him. He was accessible to none of his Court but at the stated hours of business and ceremony; nor was any man but the Favourite, and the creatures with whom he had garrisoned the palace, allowed to converse with the King. Affection had no share in this management.

The Princess, who was never supposed to disclose her mind with freedom, but on the single topic of her own children, had often mentioned her eldest son with contempt; and during the life of her husband had given into all his partiality for the Duke of York. When her views of governing by her husband were cut off, she applied to the untutored inexperience of his heir; and the first step towards the influence she meditated was by filling his mind with suspicions and ill impressions of all mankind. His uncle, the Duke of Cumberland, was made another instrument. The young Prince had a great appetite; he was asked if he wished to be as gross as his uncle? Every vice, every condescension was imputed to the Duke, that the Prince might be stimulated to avoid them.

The Favourite, who had notions of honour, and was ostentatious, endeavoured to give a loftier cast to the disposition of his pupil, though not to the disparagement of the vassalage in which he was to be kept. Lord Bute had a little reading, and affected learning. Men of genius, the arts and artists were to be countenanced. The arts might amuse the young King's solitary hours; authors might defend the measures of Government, and were sure to pay for their pensions with incense, both to their passive and active protectors. The pedantry and artifice of these shallow views served but to produce ridicule. Augustus fell asleep over drawings and medals, which were pushed before him every evening; and Mæcenas had so little knowledge, and so little taste, that his own letters grew a proverb for want of orthography; and the scribblers he countenanced were too destitute of talents to raise his character or their own. The coins of the King were the worst that had appeared for above a century; and the revenues of the Crown were so soon squandered in purchasing dependants, that architecture, the darling art of Lord Bute, was contracted from the erection of a new palace to altering a single door-case in the drawing-room at St. James's. Yet his emissaries, the Scotch, were indefatigable in coining popular sayings and sentences for the King. It was given out that he would suffer no money to be spent on elections. Circumstances that recoiled with force, when every one of those aphorisms were contradicted by practice.

But the chief engine to conciliate favour was the King's piety. The Princess, no doubt, intended it should be real, for she lived in dread of a mistress. But mankind was not inclined to think that her morals could have imprinted much devotion on the mind of her son; nor was any man the dupe of those professions but Secker, the Archbishop, who, for the first days of the reign, flattered himself with the idea of becoming first minister in a Court that hoisted the standard of religion. He was unwearied in attendance at St. James's, and in presenting bodies of clergy; and his assiduity was so bustling and assuming that, having pushed aside the Duke of Cumberland to get at the King, his Royal Highness reprimanded him with a bitter taunt. The prelate soon discovered his mistake. Nor were the Princess or the Favourite inclined to trust the King in the hands of a Churchman, whom they knew so well, and whose sanctity was as equivocal as their own.

As far as could be discerned of the King's natural disposition it was humane and benevolent. If flowing courtesy to all men was the habit of his dissimulation, at least it was so suited to his temper that no gust of passion, no words of bitterness, were ever known to break from him. He accepted services with grace and appearance of feeling; and if he forgot them with an unrestrained facility, yet he never marked his displeasure with harshness. Silence served him to bear with unwelcome ministers, or to part with them. His childhood was tinctured with obstinacy; it was adopted at the beginning of his reign, and called firmness, but did not prove to be his complexion. In truth, it would be difficult to draw his character in positive colours. He had neither passions nor activity. He resigned himself obsequiously to the government of his mother and Lord Bute; learned, and even entered with art into the lessons they inspired, but added nothing of his own. When the task was done, he relapsed into indifference and indolence till roused to the next day's part.

* * *

It must, I think, appear evident, from the scope of the reign, that the Princess Dowager and Lord Bute had assumed the reins with a fixed intention of raising the prerogative, which they called restoring it to its ancient lustre; but nothing would have induced them to specify at what period of its influence they would have been contented to have stopped. The line of Hanover having been advanced to the throne by the forfeiture of the Stuarts, could not have the confidence to demand all the power that had been claimed by that House from which they descended, whose maxims they secretly revered, and whose want of abilities they inherited. King William had been too much controlled by his parliaments to serve them for a precedent; and the beginning of this very reign had been too servilely copied from the conclusion of Queen Anne's, and too ingloriously to be fit for quotation, though the doctrines of her last Ministers were the rule on which the junto had intended to act, and did act whenever they found themselves strong enough. But, as recent provocations govern the actions of men more than maxims, it was the conduct of the later Ministers of George the Second that first inspired the Princess of Wales and her husband, Prince Frederic, with desires of emancipating themselves from such pupillage. I am persuaded that she, her husband, and her son (if the latter at first had any plan) meditated humbling the aristocracy, rather than invading liberty.

* * *

The canker had begun in the Administration of the Pelhams and Lord Hardwicke, who, at the head of a proud aristocracy of Whig Lords, had thought of nothing but establishing their own power; and who, as it suited their occasional purposes, now depressed and insulted the Crown and Royal Family, and now raised the prerogative. Their factious usurpations and insolence were even some excuse for the maxim taken up by Frederic, Prince of Wales, by the Princess Dowager, and the reigning King, of breaking that overbearing combination; and so blinded were the Pelhams by their own ambition, that they furnished the Princess with men whose principles and abilities were best suited to inspire arbitrary notions into her son, and to instruct him how to get rid of his tyrants, and establish a despotism that may end in tyranny in his descendants. Though the Princess and Lord Bute gave rashly in to those views, their passions, folly, and cowardice oftener defeated the plan than promoted it: and it was in this light only that Lord Bute ought to be acquitted of raising the prerogative. *He* rendered it contemptible; while Stone and Murray were the real sources of those discontents, which Burke sought, but never discovered. . . .[1] A few facts will evince that the Pelhams, Hardwicke, and their friends, were an aristocratic faction; that they insulted and provoked the Crown and Royal Family, and raised disgusts in them against the Whig party, at the same time planting the rankest Tories about the successor and his mother, and forcing them to throw themselves into the arms of even Jacobites.

*   *   *

Let it be observed, however, that, when I impute to the King and his mother little more than a formed design of reducing the usurped authority of the great Lords, I am far from meaning that there were no deeper designs at bottom. Lord Mansfield was by principle a tyrant; Lord Holland was bred in a monarchic school, was cruel, revengeful, daring, and subtle. Grenville, though in principle a republican, was bold, proud,

[1] A scornful reference to Burke's *Thoughts on the Causes of the Present Discontents.*

dictatorial, and so self-willed that he would have expected Liberty herself should be his first slave. The Bedford faction, except the Duke himself, were void of honour, honesty, and virtue; and the Scotch were whatever their masters wished them to be, and too envious of the English, and became too much provoked by them, not to lend all their mischievous abilities towards the ruin of a constitution, whose benefits the English had imparted to them, but did not like they should engross. All these individuals or factions, I do not doubt, accepted and fomented the disposition they found predominant in the Cabinet, as they had severally access to it; and the contradictions which the King suffered in his ill-advised measures, riveted in him a thirst of delivering himself from control, and to be above control he must be absolute. Thus on the innate desire of unbounded power in all princes, was engrafted a hate to the freedom of the subject, and therefore, whether the King set out with a plan of extending his prerogative, or adopted it, his subsequent measures, as often as he had an opportunity of directing them himself, tended to the sole object of acting by his own will. Frequent convulsions did that pursuit occasion, and heavy mortifications to himself. On the nation it heaped disgrace, and brought it to the brink of ruin; and should the event be consonant to the King's wishes of establishing the royal authority at home, it is more sure that the country will be so lowered, that the Sovereign will become as subject to the mandates of France, as any little potentate in Europe.

II. THE WHIG HISTORIANS

The Ambitious King

THOMAS ERSKINE MAY

Thomas Erskine May (1815–1886) spent his life in the service of the House of Commons, beginning at the age of sixteen as an assistant librarian and eventually becoming clerk of the house of commons. His works on history and constitutional law were rooted in his dedication to the principles of the responsibility of the crown to Parliament and of Parliament to the people. In 1847 he published his *Practical Treatise on the Law, Privileges, Proceeding, and Usages of Parliament*, and in 1854 he prepared the *Rules, Orders, and Forms of the House of Commons*. His *Constitutional History of England since the Accession of George III* should be understood primarily as an historical preface to his works on Parliament, tracing through the previous century the development of the practices and principles of his own time. As such, the work is a representative statement of the ideals and attitudes which underlay mid-Victorian parliamentary government.

THE growth of the influence of the crown, at a period in the history of this country when government by prerogative had recently been subverted, and popular rights and liberties enlarged, attests the vital power of the monarchy. At the Revolution, the arbitrary rule of the Stuart kings finally gave way to parliamentary government, with ministerial responsibility. Such a change portended the subjection of future kings to the will of Parliament; but it proved no more than a security for the observance of the law. While the exercise of the royal authority was restrained within the proper limits of the constitution, the crown was shorn of none of its ancient prerogatives; but remained, as it had ever been, the source of all power, civil and ecclesiastical, — "the fountain of honour," — the first and paramount institution of the state. Its powers, indeed, were now exercised by ministers responsible to Parliament; and the House of Commons was no longer held in awe by royal prerogative. Yet so great were the attributes of royalty, and so numerous its sources of influence, that, for more than a century after the Revolution, it prevailed over the more popular elements of the constitution. A Parliament representing the people little more than in name, and free, in great measure, from the restraint of public opinion, — which had not yet the means of being intelligently formed, or adequately expressed, — promoted the views of rival parties, rather than the interests of the people. This popular institution, designed to control the crown, was won over to its side, and shared, while it supported, its ascendency. The crown now governed with more difficulty, and was forced to use all its resources for the maintenance of its authority: but it governed as completely as ever.

Meanwhile every accession to the great-

From Thomas Erskine May, *The Constitutional History of England since the Accession of George the Third, 1760–1860*, 3 vols. (11th ed., London, 1896), vol. I, pp. 1–17.

ness of the country favoured the influence of the crown. By the increase of establishments and public expenditure, the means of patronage were multiplied. As the people grew more wealthy, considerable classes appeared in society, whose sympathies were with "the powers that be," and who coveted favours which the crown alone could bestow. And thus the very causes which ultimately extended the power of the people, for a long time served to enlarge the influence of the crown.

Vast and various were the sources of this influence. The crown bestowed everything which its subjects most desired to obtain; honours, dignities, places and preferments. Such a power reached all classes, and swayed constituents, as well as Parliaments. The House of Lords has ever been more closely associated with the crown and its interests than the House of Commons. The nobles of every land are the support and ornament of the court; and in England they are recognized as an outwork of the monarchy, — a defence against the democratic elements of our institutions. The entire body is the creation of the crown. The temporal peers, or their ancestors, have all been ennobled by royal favour: many have been raised to a higher dignity in the peerage; and others aspire to such an elevation. A peerage of the United Kingdom is an object of ambition to Scotch and Irish peers. The spiritual lords owe their dignity to the crown, and look up to the same source of power for translation to more important sees. Nearly all the highest honours and offices are engrossed by the nobility. The most powerful duke, who has already enjoyed every other honour, still aspires to the Order of the Garter. The lord-lieutenancy of a county, — an office of feudal grandeur, — confers distinction and influence, of which the noblest are justly proud. Other great appointments in the state and royal household are enjoyed exclusively by peers and their families; while a large proportion of the state patronage is dispensed by their hands. Their rank also brings them within the immediate reach of court favour

and social courtesies, by which the most eminent peers naturally become the personal friends of the reigning sovereign. Accordingly, with some rare exceptions, the House of Lords has always ranged itself on the side of the crown. It has supported the king himself against his own ministers; it has yielded up its convictions at his word; and where party connections have brought it into conflict with a ministry enjoying the confidence of the crown, its opposition has been feeble or compliant. Nor has its general support of the throne been inconsistent with the theory of the constitution.

The Commons, on the other hand, representing the people, are assumed to be independent of the crown, and jealous of its influence. How far these have been their actual characteristics, will be examined hereafter: but here it may be briefly said, that until the reform in the representation of the people in 1832, the counties were mainly under the influence of great and noble families — as they still are, to a considerable extent: a large proportion of the boroughs were either the absolute property of peers and their connections, or entirely under their control; while in many other boroughs the interest of the government was paramount at elections. The cities and large towns alone had any pretensions to independence. Except on rare occasions, when all classes were animated by a strong public opinion, the representation of the people and popular interests was a constitutional theory, rather than an active political force. Had there been no party distinctions, there could scarcely have been an ostensible opposition to any ministers whom the king might have chosen to appoint. Members of Parliament sought eagerly the patronage of the crown. Services at elections, and support in Parliament, were rewarded with peerages, baronetcies, offices and pensions. Such rewards were openly given: the consideration was avowed. There were other secret rewards of a grosser character, which need not here be noticed. Nor were constituents beyond the reach of the same influence. The collection and expenditure of an enormous and continually increasing public revenue provided inferior places, — almost without number, — which were dispensed on the recommendation of members supporting the government. Hence to vote with the ministers of the day was the sure road to advancement: to vote against them was certain neglect and proscription.

To these sources of influence must be added the loyalty of the British people. He must indeed be a bad king, whom the people do not love. Equally remarkable are their steady obedience to the law, and respect for authority. Their sympathies are generally on the side of the government. In a good cause their active support may be relied upon; and even in a bad cause, their prejudices have more often been enlisted in favour of the government than against it. How great then, for good or for evil, were the powers of a British sovereign and his ministers. The destinies of a great people depended upon their wisdom, nearly as much as if they had wielded arbitrary power.

But while these various sources of influence continued to maintain the political ascendency of the crown, the personal share of the sovereign in the government of the country was considerably restricted. William III, the most able statesman of his day, while representing the principles of the Revolution, was yet his own minister for foreign affairs, conducted negotiations abroad, and commanded armies in the field. But henceforward a succession of sovereigns less capable than William, and of ministers gifted with extraordinary ability and force of character, rapidly reduced to practice the theory of ministerial responsibility.

The government of the state was conducted, throughout all its departments, by ministers responsible to Parliament for every act of their administration, — without whose advice no act could be done — who could be dismissed for incapacity or failure, and impeached for political crimes; and who resigned when their advice was disregarded by the crown, or their policy disapproved by Parliament. With ministers thus responsible, "the king could do no wrong." The Stuarts had strained prerogative so far, that it had twice snapped asunder in their hands. They had exercised it personally, and were held personally responsible for its exercise. One had paid the penalty with his head: another with his crown; and their family had been proscribed for ever. But now, if the prerogative was strained, ministers were condemned, and not the king. If the people cried out against the government, — instead of a revolution, there was merely a change of ministry. Instead of dangerous conflicts between the crown and Parliament, there succeeded struggles between rival parties for parliamentary majorities; and the successful party wielded all the power of the state. Upon ministers, therefore, devolved the entire burthen of public affairs: they relieved the crown of its cares and perils, but, at the same time, they appropriated nearly all its authority. The king reigned, but his ministers governed.

To an ambitious prince, this natural result of constitutional government could not fail to be distasteful; but the rule of the House of Hanover had hitherto been peculiarly favourable to its development. With George I and George II, Hanoverian politics had occupied the first place in their thoughts and affections. Of English politics, English society, and even the English language, they knew little. The troublesome energies of Parliament were an enigma to them; and they cheerfully acquiesced in the ascendency of able ministers who had suppressed rebellions, and crushed pretenders to their crown, — who had triumphed over parliamentary opposition and had borne all the burthen of the government. Left to the indulgence of their own personal tastes, — occupied by frequent visits to the land of their birth, — by a German court, favourites and mistresses, — they were not anxious to engage, more than was necessary, in the turbulent contests of a constitutional government. Having lent their name and authority to competent ministers, they acted upon their advice, and aided them by all the means at the disposal of the court.

This authority had fallen to the lot of ministers connected with the Whig party, to whom the House of Hanover mainly owed its throne. The most eminent of the Tories had been tainted with Jacobite principles and connections; and some of them had even plotted for the restoration of the Stuarts. From their ranks the Pretender had twice drawn the main body of his adherents. The Whigs, indeed, could not lay claim to exclusive loyalty: nor were the Tories generally obnoxious to the charge of disaffection: but the Whigs having acquired a superior title to the favours of the court, and being once admitted to office, contrived, — by union amongst themselves, by borough interests, and by their monopoly of the influence of the crown, — to secure an ascendency in Parliament which, for nearly fifty years, was almost unassailable. Until the fall of Sir Robert Walpole the Whigs had been compact and united; and their policy had generally been to carry out, in practice, the principles of the Revolution. When no longer under the guidance of that minister, their coherence, as a party, was disturbed; and they became divided into families and cliques. To use the words of Lord John Russell, this "was the age of small factions." The distinctive policy of the party was lost in the personal objects of its leaders; but political power still remained in the same hands; and, by alliances rather than by union, the "great Whig families," and others admitted to a share of their power, continued to engross all the high offices of state, and to distribute among their personal adherents the entire patronage of the crown.

The young king, George III, on succeeding to the throne, regarded with settled jealousy the power of his ministers, as an encroachment on his own; and resolved to break it down. His personal popularity was such as to facilitate the execution of this design. Well knowing that the foreign ex-

traction of his predecessors had repressed the affections of their people, he added, with his own hand, to the draft of his first speech to Parliament, the winning phrase, "Born and educated in this country, I glory in the name of Briton." The Stuarts were now the aliens, and not the Hanoverian king. A new reign, also, was favourable to the healing of political differences, and to the fusion of parties. In Scotland, a few fanatical non-jurors may still have grudged their allegiance to an uncovenanted king. But none of the young king's subjects had plotted against his throne; and few could be suspected of adherence to the fallen cause of the Stuarts, which had been hopelessly abandoned since the rebellion of 1745. The close phalanx of the Whig party had already been broken; and Mr. Pitt had striven to conciliate the Tories, and put an end to the bitter feuds by which the kingdom had been distracted. No party was now in disgrace at court: but Whigs, Tories, and Jacobites thronged to St. James's, and vied with each other in demonstrations of loyalty and devotion.

The king was naturally ambitious, and delighted in the active exercise of power; and his education, — otherwise neglected, — had raised his estimate of the personal rights of a king in the government of his country. So far back as 1752, complaints had been made that the prince was surrounded by Jacobite preceptors, who were training him in arbitrary principles of government. At that time, these complaints were discredited as factious calumnies: but the political views of the king, on his accession to the throne, appear to confirm the suspicions entertained concerning his early education.

His mother, the Princess Dowager of Wales, — herself ambitious and fond of power, — had derived her views of the rights and authority of a sovereign from German courts; and encouraged the prince's natural propensities by the significant advice of "George, be king." Lord Waldegrave, who had been for some time governor to the prince, describes him as "full of princely prejudices contracted in the nursery, and improved by the society of bedchamber-women and pages of the back-stairs."

His groom of the stole, Lord Bute, — afterwards so notorious as his minister, — had also given the young prince instruction in the theory of the British constitution; and knowing little more than the princess herself, of the English people and government, had taught him that his own honour, and the interests of the country, required the extension of his personal influence, and a more active exercise of his prerogatives. The chief obstacle to this new policy of the court was found in the established authority of responsible ministers, upheld by party connections and parliamentary interest. Accordingly, the first object of the king and his advisers was to loosen the ties of party, and break down the confederacy of the great Whig families. The king desired to undertake personally the chief administration of public affairs, to direct the policy of his ministers, and himself to distribute the patronage of the crown. He was ambitious not only to reign, but to govern. His will was strong and resolute, his courage high, and his talent for intrigue considerable. He came to the throne determined to exalt the kingly office; and throughout his long reign he never lost sight of that paramount object.

Lord Bolingbroke had conceived the idea of a government under "a patriot king," — who should "govern as soon as he begins to reign," — who should "call into the administration such men as he can assure himself will serve on the same principles on which he intends to govern," — and who should "put himself at the head of his people in order to govern, or, more properly, to subdue all parties." But it had been no part of Lord Bolingbroke's conception, that the patriot king should suffer his favourites to stand between him and his "most able and faithful councillors." Such, however, was the scheme of George the Third.

The ministry whom the king found in possession of power at his accession, had been formed by a coalition between the Duke of Newcastle and Mr. Pitt. The former had long been the acknowledged leader of the great Whig connection, and enjoyed extended parliamentary interest: the latter, by his eloquence and statesmanship, had become the most popular and powerful of the king's subjects. The ministry also comprised the Grenville and Bedford sections of the Whig party. It was so strong in Parliament, that for some years the voice of opposition had been scarcely heard; and so long as it continued united, its position was impregnable.

But, strong as were the ministers, the king was resolved to wrest all power from their hands, and to exercise it himself. For this purpose he called to his aid the Earl of Bute, and other secret counsellors, drawn from all parties. The greater number were of the Tory party, whose views of prerogative were Jacobite. According to Horace Walpole, "they abjured their ancient master, but retained their principles." It was the king's object not merely to supplant one party, and establish another in its place, but to create a new party, faithful to himself, regarding his personal wishes, carrying out his policy, and dependent on his will. This party was soon distinguished as "the king's men," or "the king's friends." Instead of relying upon the advice of his responsible ministers, the king took counsel with this "double" or "interior cabinet." Even his first speech to Parliament was not submitted to the cabinet council. It had been drawn up by himself and Lord Bute; and when Mr. Pitt took exception to some of its expressions, the king long resisted the advice of his minister. It had been usual for ministers to rely upon the support of the crown in all their measures. They now found themselves thwarted and opposed; and the patronage, which they had regarded as their own, they saw divided by the king among his new adherents and their connections. This "influence behind the throne" was denounced by all the leading statesmen of that time, — by Mr. Grenville, Lord Chatham, the Marquess of Rockingham, the Duke of Bedford, and Mr. Burke. Occasionally denied, its existence was yet so notorious, and its agency so palpable, that historical writers of all parties, — while taking different views of its character — have not failed to acknowledge it. The bitterness with which it was assailed at the time was due, in great measure, to political jealousies, and to the king's selection of his friends from an unpopular party; but, on constitutional grounds, it was unquestionably open to the gravest objections.

A constitutional government ensures to the king a wide authority, in all the councils of the state. He chooses and dismisses his ministers; and this, — if it be his pleasure, — without the advice of any councillor. Their resolutions upon every important measure of foreign and domestic policy are submitted to his approval; and when that approval is withheld, his ministers must either abandon their policy, or resign their offices. They are responsible to the king on the one hand, and to Parliament on the other; and while they retain the confidence of the king, by administering affairs to his satisfaction, they must act upon principles, and propose measures, which they can justify to Parliament. And here is the proper limit to the king's influence. As he governs by responsible ministers, he must recognize their responsibilities. They are not his ministers only, but also the public servants of a free country. But an influence in the direction of public affairs thus limited, by no mean satisfied the ambition of the king. His courtiers represented that he was enthralled by the dominant party, which had become superior to the throne itself; and that in order to recover his just prerogative, it was necessary to break up the combination. But what was this, in effect, but to assert that the king should now be his own minister? that ministers should be chosen, not because they had the confidence of Parliament and the country, but because they were agreeable to himself, and willing to carry out his policy? — And this was the true object of the king. It will be seen that when ministers, not of his own

choice, were in office, he plotted and manœuvred until he overthrew them; and when he had succeeded in establishing his friends in office, he forced upon them the adoption of his own policy.

The king's tactics were fraught with danger, as well to the crown itself as to the constitutional liberties of the people: but his personal conduct and character have sometimes been judged with too much severity. That he was too fond of power for a constitutional monarch, none will now be found to deny: that he sometimes resorted to crafty expedients, unworthy of a king, even his admirers must admit. But he had kingly virtues, — piety, courage, constancy, and patriotism. With a narrow understanding and obstinate prejudices, he yet laboured, honestly, for the good government of his country. If he loved power, he did not shrink from its cares and toil. If he delighted in being the active ruler of his people, he devoted himself to affairs of state, even more laboriously than his ministers. If he was jealous of the authority of the crown, he was not less jealous of the honour and greatness of his people. A just recognition of the personal merits of the king himself, enables us to judge more freely of the constitutional tendency and results of his policy.

To revert to a polity under which kings had governed, and ministers had executed their orders, was in itself a dangerous retrogression in the principles of constitutional government. If the crown, and not its ministers, had governed, how could the former do no wrong, and the latter be responsible? If ministers were content to accept responsibility without power, the crown could not escape its share of blame. Hence the chief safeguard of the monarchy was endangered. But the liberties of the people were exposed to greater peril than the crown. Power proceeding from the king, and exercised by himself in person, is irreconcilable with popular government. It constitutes the main distinction between an absolute and a constitutional monarchy. The best and most enlightened of kings, governing from above, will press his own policy upon his subjects. Choosing his ministers from considerations personal to himself, — directing their acts, — upholding them as his own servants, — resenting attacks upon them as disrespectful to himself, — committed to their measures, and resolved to enforce them, — viewing men and things from the elevation of a court, instead of sharing the interests and sympathies of the people, — how can he act in harmony with popular influences?

The system of government which George III found in operation was indeed imperfect. The influence of the crown, as exercised by ministers, prevailed over the more popular elements of the constitution. The great nobles were too powerful. A Parliament, without adequate representation of the people, and uncontrolled by public opinion, was generally subservient to ministers: but with all its defects, it was still a popular institution. If not freely elected by the people, it was yet composed of men belonging to various classes of society, and sharing their interests and feelings. The statesmen, who were able by their talents and influence to command its confidence, became the ministers of the crown; and power thus proceeded from below, instead of from above. The country was governed by its ablest men, and not by favourites of the court. The proper authority of Parliament was recognised; and nothing was wanting in the theory of constitutional government, but an improved constitution of Parliament itself. This system, however, the king was determined to subvert. He was jealous of ministers who derived their authority from Parliament rather than from himself, and of the parliamentary organisation which controlled his power. The policy which he adopted, and its results, are among the most critical events in the history of the crown.

The Obstinate King

W. E. H. LECKY

W. E. H. Lecky (1838–1903) was born and educated in Ireland, and throughout his life he maintained a strong interest in Ireland. His early works were studies of the origin and decline of traditional Christian morality, and near the end of his life he surveyed the growth of democracy, viewing with concern the threat which it posed to his ideals of personal liberty and representative government. He served in Parliament from 1895 to 1902, where he showed special interest in Irish affairs. He died in 1903, old and full of honors, after a long, active, and productive life.

Lecky's greatest work is his *History of England in the Eighteenth Century*, which he worked on for nineteen years. The work was mainly political, but Lecky included long sections on society, religion, and manners. He gave much attention to imperial questions, especially Ireland, to which he gave full and sympathetic treatment. American historians praised the fairness of his treatment of the American Revolution. In its amplitude, its leisured pace, its rich detail, its elegant style, its lofty (and often sententious) spirit and its assured tone, Lecky's *History of England in the Eighteenth Century* is a splendid example of the Victorian mind and a work which has found a place among the classics of English historiography.

WHEN George II died, on October 25, 1760, his grandson and successor had but just completed his twenty-second year. The life of the young Prince had hitherto been very unsuitable for the task he was to fulfil. Since his thirteenth year, when his father died, he had lived entirely with his mother, and he exhibited during his whole career the characteristic merits and defects of a female education. His mother was a woman of a somewhat hard, reserved, and tortuous character, with few friendships and several bitter enmities; with a power of concealing her true sentiments which baffled even those who came in closest connection with her; strict in the observance of her religious duties, and in her care of her nine children; eminently discreet in her dealings with a bad husband and a jealous father-in-law; deeply imbued with the narrow prejudices of a small German Court, fond of power, unamiable, and somewhat soured by adversity. The early death of her husband had deprived her of the prospect of a crown, and although after his death Leicester House[1] ceased to be a centre of active opposition, the old King looked upon both the Princess and his grandchild with jealousy, and they had in consequence little intercourse with the Court circle, with the Whig ministers, and even with the other members of the royal family. The education of the young Prince was feebly and fitfully conducted; and it is remarkable that among his preceptors Scott had been recommended by Bolingbroke, while Stone had been suspected of Jacobitism. They appear to have discharged their functions very ill; for George III was always singularly deficient in literary culture. Lord Waldegrave, who was much the ablest of his governors, described him as a

---

[1] Leicester House was the residence of the Prince of Wales. The name was applied to the opposition groups which often gathered around the heir to the throne.

From William Edward Hartpole Lecky, *A History of England in the Eighteenth Century*, 8 vols. (London, 1883), vol. III, pp. 10–23.

boy of respectable abilities, but great constitutional indolence; scrupulous, dutiful, ignorant of evil, and sincerely pious, but neither generous nor frank; harsh in his judgments of others, with strong prejudices, indomitable obstinacy, and great command over his passions, exceedingly tenacious of his resentments, and exhibiting them chiefly by prolonged fits of sullenness. His indolence he succeeded in completely overcoming, but the other lines of this not very pleasing picture continued during his whole life. He mixed very little in the world — scarcely at all with the young nobility. His mother said that their lax manners would probably corrupt her son. Her enemies declared that the real explanation of this strange seclusion was her own insatiable avarice of power, which made her wish beyond all things to establish a complete ascendency over his mind, and to withdraw him from every influence that could rival her own. Like most members of German royal families, she exaggerated the prerogative of monarchy to the highest degree, and her favourite exhortation, "George, be a king!" is said to have left a deep impression on the mind of her son. The most important figure in the small circle was John, Earl of Bute, a Scotch nobleman who had held an office in the household of Frederick, Prince of Wales, had lived after his death for some years a life of more than common retirement in Scotland, and, on the establishment of the household of the young Prince, had been placed at the head of it as Groom of the Stole. He was a man of some literary and artistic taste, but of very limited talents, entirely inexperienced in public business, arrogant, reserved, and unpopular in his temper, and with extreme views of the legitimate powers of royalty. The very confidential relations of Bute with the Princess gave rise to a scandal which was widely spread and generally believed. He became the chief adviser or instructor of her son, and strengthened in his mind those plans for the emancipation of the royal authority

which George III pursued steadily throughout his whole life.

The new sovereign came to the throne amid an enthusiasm such as England had hardly seen since Charles II restored the monarchy. By the common consent of all parties the dynastic contest was regarded as closed, and after two generations of foreign and unsympathetic rulers, the nation, which has always been peculiarly intolerant of strangers, accepted with delight an English king. The favourable impression was still further confirmed when the more salient points of the private character of the King became generally understood. Simple, regular, and abstemious in all his tastes and habits, deeply religious without affectation or enthusiasm, a good son, a faithful husband, a kind master, and (except when he had met with gross ingratitude) an affectionate father, he exhibited through his whole reign, and in a rare perfection, that type of decorous and domestic virtue which the English middle classes most highly prize. The proclamation against immorality with which he began his reign; the touching piety with which, at his coronation, he insisted on putting aside his crown when receiving the sacrament; his rebuke to a Court preacher who had praised him in a sermon; his suppression of Sunday levees; his discouragement of gambling at Court; his letter of remonstrance to an Archbishop of Canterbury who had allowed balls in his palace; his constant attendance and reverential manner at religious services; his solemn and pious resignation under great private misfortunes, contrasted admirably with the open immorality of his father, his grandfather, and his great-grandfather, and with the outrageous licentiousness of his own brothers and of his own sons. He never sought for popularity; but he had many of the kingly graces, and many of the national tastes that are most fitted to obtain it. He went through public ceremonies with much dignity, and although his manner in private was hurried and confused, it was kind and homely, and not without a certain unaffected grace. Unlike his two predecessors, he was emphatically a gentleman, and he possessed to a rare degree the royal art of enhancing small favours by a gracious manner and a few well-chosen words. His country tastes, his love of field-sports, his keen interest in the great public schools, endeared him to large classes of his subjects; and, though he was neither brilliant nor witty, several of his terse and happy sayings are still remembered. He was also a very brave man. In the Wilkes riots, in 1769, when his palace was attacked; in the Lord George Gordon riots, in 1780, when his presence of mind contributed largely to save London; in 1786, when a poor madwoman attempted to stab him at the entrance of St. James's Palace; in 1795, when he was assailed on his way to Parliament; in 1800, when he was fired at in a theatre, he exhibited the most perfect composure amid danger. His habit in dating his letters, of marking, not only the day, but the hour and the minute in which he wrote, illustrates not unhappily the microscopic attention which he paid to every detail of public business, and which was the more admirable because his natural tendency was towards sloth. In matters that were not connected with his political prejudices, his sincere appreciation of piety and his desire to do good sometimes overcame his religious bigotry and his hatred of change. Thus he always spoke with respect of the Methodists, and especially of Lady Huntingdon; he supported Howard, and subscribed to a statue in his honour; he supported the Lancaster system of education, though Lancaster was a Dissenter, and was looked upon with disfavour by the bishops; he encouraged the movement for Sunday-schools. He was sincerely desirous of doing his duty, and deeply attached to his country, although stronger feelings often interfered both with his conscientiousness and with his patriotism.

It is not surprising that a sovereign of whom all this may be truly said should have obtained much respect and admiration; and it must be added that, in his hatred of innovation and in his vehement anti-American, anti-Catholic, and anti-Gallican feelings, he represented the sentiments of large sections — perhaps of the majority — of his people. The party which he drew from its depression has naturally revered his memory, and old age, and blindness, and deafness, and deprivation of reason, and the base ingratitude of two sons, have cast a deep pathos over his closing years.

All these things have contributed very naturally to throw a delusive veil over the political errors of a sovereign of whom it may be said without exaggeration, that he inflicted more profound and enduring injuries upon his country than any other modern English king. Ignorant, narrow-minded, and arbitrary, with an unbounded confidence in his own judgment and an extravagant estimate of his prerogative, resolved at all hazards to compel his ministers to adopt his own views, or to undermine them if they refused, he spent a long life in obstinately resisting measures which are now almost universally admitted to have been good, and in supporting measures which are as universally admitted to have been bad. He espoused with passionate eagerness the American quarrel; resisted obstinately the measures of conciliation by which at one time it might easily have been stifled; envenomed it by his glaring partisanship, and protracted it for several years, in opposition to the wish and to the advice even of his own favourite and responsible minister. He took the warmest personal interest in the attempts that were made, in the matter of general warrants, to menace the liberty of the subject, and in the case of the Middlesex election to abridge the electoral rights of constituencies, and in the other paltry, violent, and arbitrary measures by which the country was inflamed and Wilkes was converted into a hero. The last instance of an English officer deprived of his regiment for his vote in Parliament was due to the personal intervention of the King; and the ministers whom he most warmly favoured were guilty of an amount and audacity of corruption which is probably unequalled in the parliamentary history of England. All the measures that were carried or attempted with the object of purifying the representative body — the publication of debates, the alteration of the mode of trying contested elections, the reduction of sinecures and pensions, the enlargement of the constituencies — were contrary to the wishes of the King. Although his income during the greater part of his reign was little less than a million a year, although his Court was parsimonious to a fault, and his hospitality exceedingly restricted, and although he succeeded to a considerable sum that had been saved by his predecessor, he accumulated in the course of his reign debts to the amount of no less than 3,398,-061*l.*; and there can be little doubt that contemporary public opinion was right in attributing a great part of these debts to his expenditure in parliamentary or electoral corruption.

*   *   *

The root, however, of his great errors lay in his determination to restore the royal power to a position wholly different from that which it occupied in the reign of his predecessor; and this design was in many respects more plausible than is now generally admitted. Every functionary has a natural tendency to magnify his office, and when George III ascended the throne he found his position as an hereditary constitutional sovereign almost unique in the world. In France, in Spain, in Austria, in the smallest principality in Germany, the sovereign was hardly less absolute than in Russia or Turkey. And the power of the English sovereign had for many years been steadily declining, and the limitations to which he was practically subject went far beyond the mere letter of the law. The time had indeed long passed when Elizabeth directed her Parliaments to abstain from discussing matters of state, and when

James I declared that, "as it is atheism and blasphemy in a creature to dispute what the Deity may do, so it is presumption and sedition in a subject to dispute what a king may do in the height of his power;" but even after the Revolution, William III had been a great political power, and Anne, though a weak and foolish woman, had exercised no small amount of personal influence. What the position of the English sovereign was in the eyes of the English Church was sufficiently shown by the long series of theologians who proclaimed in the most emphatic terms that he possessed a Divine right, different, not only in degree but in kind, from that of every other power in the State; that he was the representative or vicegerent of the Deity; that resistance to him was in all cases a sin. The language of English law was less unqualified, but still it painted his authority in very different colours from those which an historian of George I or of George II would have used. The "Commentaries" of Blackstone were not published till George III had been for some time on the throne; but Bute had obtained a considerable portion of them in manuscript from the author, for the purpose of instructing the Prince in the principles of the Constitution. "The King of England," in the words of Blackstone, "is not only the chief, but properly the sole magistrate of the nation, all others acting by commission from and in due subordination to him." "He may reject what bills, may make what treaties . . . may pardon what offences he pleases, unless when the Constitution hath expressly, or by evident consequence, laid down some exception or boundary." He has the sole power of regulating fleets and armies, of manning all forts and other places of strength within the realm, of making war and peace, of conferring honours, offices, and privileges. He governs the kingdom: statesmen, who administer affairs, are only his ministers.

It is not surprising that the contrast between such language and the actual position of George II during the greater part of his reign should have vividly impressed a young sovereign surrounded by Tory followers, and naturally extremely tenacious of power, or that he should have early resolved to bend all his faculties to the task of emancipating his office from the restrictions that surrounded it. The period of his accession was in some respects exceedingly propitious to his design. Among the causes of the depression of royalty one of the most obvious and important had been the long exclusion from office of that great Tory party which naturally exalts most highly the royal prerogative.

*   *   *

The propriety of breaking down the system of exclusion seemed manifest. The Tory sentiment of the country had long found no adequate expression in the Government. The party which carried with it the genuine sympathies both of the country gentry and of the country clergy had been so discouraged that after the death of Bolingbroke and of the Prince of Wales it was scarcely represented in Parliament, and its political eclipse had been followed by a great increase both of oligarchical influence and of corruption. There was something manifestly unhealthy in the continuance during many years, of a Government like that of Walpole, which was supported chiefly by a majority of members of nomination boroughs in opposition to the large majority of the county votes; and nothing but the wisdom and moderation with which the Whig party used their ascendency could have repressed serious discontent in the country. Bolingbroke, in works which seem to have suggested the policy of George III, had strongly urged the necessity of disregarding the old party distinctions, and building up the royal authority on their decay. Carteret, after the fall of Walpole, had designed a mixed ministry, in which Tories as well as Whigs could be admitted largely to power. Pitt had long chafed bitterly against the system of government by connection, and it was noticed that although the higher offices in the Gov-

ernment were still occupied exclusively by Whigs, the country party, who had remained sullenly indifferent to preceding Governments, rallied warmly around him, and that in his militia appointments he entirely overlooked the distinction of Whig and Tory.

The object of Pitt was to check the corruption that prevailed and to extend the area of patriotic feeling. The object of George III and of the little group of politicians who surrounded and counselled him was very different, but their means were in some respects the same. In order to estimate their policy it is necessary in the first place to form a clear conception of their aims and methods. It is probable that Burke, in the famous pamphlet in which he described the condition of English politics in the first years of George III, considerably exaggerated the systematic and elaborate character of the plan that was adopted, but its leading features are sufficiently plain. "Prerogative," as Horace Walpole said, had once more "become a fashionable word," the Divine right of kings was once again continually preached from the pulpit, and the Court party never concealed their conviction that the monarchy in the preceding reign had fallen into an essentially false position, and that it should be the first object of the new sovereign to restore it to vigour. They had, however, no wish to restrict or override the authority of Parliament, or to adopt any means which were not legal and parliamentary. Their favourite cries were abolition of government by party or connection, abolition of corruption at elections, emancipation of the sovereign from ministerial tyranny. No class of politicians were to be henceforth absolutely excluded, but at the same time no class or connection were to be allowed to dictate their policy to the King. The aristocracy, it was said, had obtained an exaggerated place in the Constitution. A few great families, who had been the leading supporters of the Revolution, who were closely connected by family relationships, by friendship, by long and systematic political co-operation, had come to form a single coherent body possessing so large an amount of borough patronage and such vast and various ramifications of influence, that they were practically the rulers of the country. This phalanx was beyond all things to be broken up. If a great nobleman consented to detach himself from it and to enter into new combinations; if on a change of ministry subordinate officials were content to abandon their leaders and to retain their places, such conduct was to be warmly encouraged. The system of divided administrations which had existed under William and Anne was to be revived. The ministers were to be as much as possible confined to their several departments; they were to be drawn from many different connections and schools of policy, and they were not to be suffered to form a coherent and homogeneous whole. The relations of the Crown to the ministry were to be changed. For a considerable time the Treasury, the Ecclesiastical patronage, the Cornish boroughs, and all the other sources of influence which belonged nominally to the Crown had been, with few exceptions, at the disposal of the minister, and were employed to strengthen his administration. They were now to be in a great degree withdrawn from his influence, and to be employed in maintaining in Parliament a body of men whose political attachment centred in the King alone, who looked to him alone for promotion, who, though often holding places in the Government, were expected rather to control than to support it, and, if it diverged from the policy which was personally acceptable to the King, to conspire against it and overthrow it. A Crown influence was thus to be established in Parliament as well as a ministerial influence, and it was hoped that it would turn the balance of parties and accelerate the downfall of any administration which was not favoured by the King.

There were many sources from which "the King's friends," as this interest was very invidiously called, might be recruited. Crown and Court patronage was extrava-gantly redundant, and it was certain in the corrupt condition of Parliament that many politicians would prefer to attach themselves to the permanent source of power rather than to transitory administrations. The popularity of the King strengthened the party. The Tories, who resented their long exclusion from power, and who recognised in the young sovereign a Tory king, supported it in a body; the divisions and jealousies among the Whig nobles made it tolerably certain that some would be soon detached from their old connections and would gather round the new standard, and the personal influence of the sovereign over the leading politicians was sufficient to secure in most ministries at least one member who was content to draw his inspiration from him alone.

It must be remembered, too, that the conception of the Cabinet as a body of statesmen who were in thorough political agreement, and were jointly responsible for all the measures they proposed, was still in its early stage, and was by no means fully or universally recognised. A great step had been taken towards its attainment on the accession of George I., when the principle was adopted of admitting only the members of a single party into the Government. The administration of Walpole, in unity, discipline, and power, was surpassed by few of the present century. After the downfall of that administration the Whigs defeated the attempt of the King's favourite statesman to mix the Government with Tories, and a joint resignation of the Government in 1746 obliged the King to break finally with Bath and Granville, and admit Pitt to his councils. But on the other hand, the lax policy of Pelham and the personal weakness of Newcastle had led to great latitude and violent divergences of policy in the Cabinet which they formed. Fox and Hardwicke, in the debates on the Marriage Act, inveighed against one another with the utmost bitterness, though the one was Secretary of State and the other Chancellor in the same Government. Fox and Pitt made their colleagues, Murray, Newcastle, and Robinson, the objects of their constant attacks, and these examples rendered it more easy for the King to carry out his favourite policy of a divided Cabinet.

A very remarkable pamphlet, called "Seasonable Hints from an Honest Man on the new Reign and the new Parliament," appeared in 1761, defending the new system of government, and it soon attracted much attention from the fact that it was understood to be the composition of no less a person than Lord Bath, the old rival of Walpole and the old colleague of Carteret.[2] The question, the writer said, for the sovereign to determine was, "Whether he is to content himself with the shadow of royalty while a set of undertakers for his business intercept his immediate communication with his people, and make use of the legal prerogatives of their master to establish the illegal claims of factitious oligarchy." He complains that "a cabal of ministers had been allowed to erect themselves into a fourth estate, to check, to control, to influence, nay, to enslave the others;" that it had become usual "to urge the necessity of the King submitting to give up the management of his affairs and the exclusive disposal of all his employments to some ministers, or set of ministers, who, by uniting together, and backed by their numerous dependents, may be able to carry on the measures of Government;" that "ministerial combinations to engross power and invade the closet," were nothing less than a "scheme of putting the sovereign in lead-

ing-strings," and that their result had been the monstrous corruption of Parliament and the strange spectacle of "a King of England unable to confer the smallest employment unless on the recommendation and with the consent of his ministers." He trusts that the new King will put an end to this system by showing "his resolution to break all factious connections and confederacies." Already he has "placed in the most honourable stations near his own person, some who have not surely owed their place to ministerial importunity, because they have always opposed ministerial influence," and by steadily pursuing this course, the true ideal of the Constitution will be attained, "in which the ministers will depend on the Crown, not the Crown on the ministers." But to attain this end it was necessary that the basis of the Government should be widened, the proscription of the Tories abolished, and the sovereign enabled to select his servants from all sections of politicians. "Does any candid and intelligent man seriously believe that at this time there subsists any party distinction amongst us that is not merely nominal? Are not the Tories friends of the royal family? Have they not long ago laid aside their aversion to the Dissenters? Do they not think the Toleration and Establishment both necessary parts of the Constitution? and can a Whig distinguish these from his own principles?" One glorious result of the new system of government the writer confidently predicts. With the destruction of oligarchical power the reign of corruption would terminate, and undue influence in Parliament was never likely to be revived.

[2] Written by John Douglas, later Bishop of Salisbury, but expressing the ideas of the Earl of Bath (William Pulteney).

III. THE NAMIER SCHOOL

A Much Maligned Ruler

SIR LEWIS NAMIER

Sir Lewis Namier (1888–1960) was born of a Polish-Jewish family, and received his university education at Oxford. He made it his task to sweep away the uncriticized assumptions and unevaluated opinions which had become the basis of the accepted interpretation of the reign of George III. His first major work, *The Structure of Politics at the Accession of George III* appeared in 1929, to be followed in 1930 by *England in the Age of the American Revolution*. The former was a rigorous examination of the House of Commons and the operations of parliamentary politics, while the latter, despite its broad title, was a detailed study of politics from 1760 to 1762, centering on the personalities of George III, Bute, Newcastle and Pitt.

With the rise of Hitlerism, Namier became passionately absorbed in the fate of European Jewry and the coming cataclysm in central Europe. Not until after the war did he return to his studies of eighteenth century England. The two essays reprinted here are a product of this period of his life. The major work of his later years was the great *History of Parliament*, which is intended to give biographical information concerning every member of Parliament, together with analyses of parliamentary groups and connections. When, if ever, this vast project is completed, it will be a fitting memorial to this most influential of modern historians of eighteenth century England.

T HERE were three large pictures of George III at the exhibition of Royal Portraits arranged by the Academy of Arts in the spring of 1953. Looking at the first, by Reynolds, painted when the King was 41, I was struck by the immaturity of expression. The second, by Lawrence, painted in 1792 at the age of 54, depicts him in Garter robes; face and posture seem to attempt in a naive, ineffective, and almost engaging manner to live up to a grandeur which the sitter feels incumbent on him. The third, by Strochling, painted in November 1807 at the age of nearly 70, shows a sad old man, looking dimly at a world in which he has no pleasure, and which he soon will not be able to see or comprehend.

A picture in a different medium of the King and his story presents itself to the student when in the Royal Archives at Windsor he surveys the papers of George III. They stand on the shelves in boxes, each marked on a white label with the year or years which it covers. The eye runs over that array, and crucial dates recall events: 1760, '65 and '67, '74 and '75, '82 and '83, 1789, '93, '96, 1802, 1805 — the series breaks off in 1810; and brown-backed volumes follow, unlabelled: they contain

Reprinted with permission of The Macmillan Company and Hamish Hamilton Ltd. from "King George III: A Study of Personality," in *Crossroads of Power* by Sir Lewis Namier (London, 1962), pp. 124–127, 130–140. Copyright 1962 by Lady Namier. Sir Lewis Namier's two major works on the period are *The Structure of Politics at the Accession of George III* (2nd ed., London, 1957) and *England in the Age of the American Revolution* (2nd ed., London, 1961).

the medical reports on a man shut off from time, which means the world and its life.

Fate had made George III ruler when kings were still expected to govern; and his active reign covered half a century during which the American conflict posed the problem of Imperial relations, while at home political practice constantly ran up against the contradiction inherent in the then much belauded "mixed form of government:" personal monarchy served by Ministers whose tenure of office was contested in Parliament. Neither the Imperial nor the constitutional problem could have been solved in the terms in which the overwhelming majority of the politically minded public in this country considered them at the time; but George III has been blamed ever since for not having thought of Dominion status and parliamentary government when constitutional theory and the facts of the situation as yet admitted of neither.

In the catalogue, *Kings and Queens,* on sale at the exhibition, the introduction dealing with the reign of George III gave the traditional view of his reign:

Conscientious and ambitious, he tried to restore the political influence of the Crown, but his intervention ended with the humiliating American War of Independence.

Conscientious he certainly was, painstakingly, almost painfully, conscientious. But was he ambitious? Did he try to exercise powers which his predecessors had relinquished, or claim an influence which was not universally conceded to him? And was it the assertion of Royal, and not of Parliamentary, authority over America which brought on the conflict and disrupted the First British Empire?

Let us place ourselves in March 1782. Dismal, humiliating failure has turned public opinion, and the House of Commons is resolved to cut losses and abandon the struggle; it is all over; Lord North's government has fallen; and the King is contemplating abdication. He has drafted a message to Parliament (which was never sent); here are its first two paragraphs:

His Majesty during the twenty-one years he has sate on the throne of Great Britain, has had no object so much at heart as the maintenance of the British Constitution, of which the difficulties he has at times met with from his scrupulous attachment to the rights of Parliament are sufficient proofs.

His Majesty is convinced that the sudden change of sentiments of one branch of the legislature has totally incapacitated him from either conducting the war with effect, or from obtaining any peace but on conditions which would prove destructive to the commerce as well as essential rights of the British nation.

In the first paragraph the King declares his unswerving devotion to the British Constitution, and shows himself conscious of his difficulties in America having arisen through "his scrupulous attachment to the rights of Parliament"; the second paragraph pointedly refers to the Commons as "one branch of the legislature," and gives the King's view of the American war; he is defending there the vital interests and essential rights of the British nation.

A year later, in March 1783, when faced by the necessity of accepting a Government formed by the Fox-North coalition, George III once more contemplated abdication; and in a letter (which again was never sent) he wrote to the Prince of Wales:

The situation of the times are such that I must, if I attempt to carry on the business of the nation, give up every political principle on which I have acted, which I should think very unjustifiable, as I have always attempted to act agreeable to my duty; and must form a Ministry from among men who know I cannot trust them and therefore who will not accept office without making me a kind of slave; this undoubtedly is a cruel dilemma, and leaves me but one step to take without the destruction of my principles and honour; the resigning my Crown, my dear Son to you, quitting this my native country for ever and returning to the dominions of my forefathers.

Your difficulties will not be the same. You

have never been in a situation to form any political system, therefore, are open to adopt what the times may make necessary; and no set of men can ever have offended you or made it impossible for you to employ them.

Alongside this consider the following passage from a letter which George III wrote on 26 December 1783, after having dismissed the Coalition and while he was trying to rally support for the newly formed Administration of the younger Pitt:

The times are of the most serious nature, the political struggle is not as formerly between two factions for power; but it is no less than whether a desperate faction shall not reduce the Sovereign to a mere tool in its hands: though I have too much principle ever to infringe the rights of others, yet that must ever equally prevent my submitting to the Executive power being in any other hands, than where the Constitution has placed it. I therefore must call on the assistance of every honest man . . . to support Government on the present most critical occasion.

Note in these two passages the King's honest conviction that he has always attempted to do his duty; that he has been mindful not to infringe the rights of others; but that it would be equally wrong in him to submit "to the Executive power being in any other hands, than where the Constitution has placed it." And while I do not for a moment suggest that these things could not have been done in a happier manner, I contend that the King's statements quoted above are substantially correct.

In the eighteenth century, a proper balance between King, Lords, and Commons, that is, the monarchical, aristocratic, and representative elements of the Constitution acting as checks on each other, was supposed to safeguard the property and privileges, the lives and liberty of the subjects. Single-Chamber government would have been no less abhorrent to the century than Royal autocracy. The Executive was the King's as truly as it is now of the President in the United States; he, too, had to choose his Ministers: but from among Parliamentary leaders. And while aspirants to office swore by the "independency" of the Crown and disclaimed all wish to force themselves on the King, if left out they did their level best to embarrass and upset their successful rivals. The technique of Parliamentary opposition was fully established long before its most essential aim, which is to force a change of government, was recognized as legitimate; and because that aim could not be avowed in its innocent purity, deadly dangers threatening the Constitution, nay the life of the country, had to be alleged for justification. Robert Walpole as "sole Minister" was accused of arrogating to himself the powers of both King and Parliament; the very tame Pelhams of keeping George II "in fetters;" Bute, who bore the name of Stuart, of "raising the standard of Royal prerogative;" and George III of ruling not through the Ministers of his own choice whom he avowed in public, but through a hidden gang of obscure and sinister "King's friends." It is obviously impossible here to trace the origin and growth of that story, or to disprove it by establishing the true facts of the transactions to which it has become attached — it was a figment so beautifully elaborated by Burke's fertile imagination that the Rockinghams themselves finished by believing it, and it grew into an obsession with them. In reality the constitutional practice of George III differed little from that of George I and George II. William Wyndham was proscribed by the first two Georges as a dangerous Jacobite, and C. J. Fox by the third as a dangerous Jacobin; while the elder Pitt was long kept out by both George II and George III on personal grounds. But for some the Royal veto and Royal influence in politics lose their sting if exercised in favour of successful monopolists in Whiggery.

I go one step further: in the eighteenth century the King had to intervene in politics and was bound to exercise his political influence, for the party system, which is the basis of Parliamentary government, did not exist. Of the House of Commons itself probably less than half thought and acted in party terms. About one-third of the House consisted of Members who looked to the King for guidance and for permanency of employment: epigoni of earlier Courts or forerunners of the modern Civil Service; and if they thus pursued their own interest, there is no reason to treat them as more corrupt than if they had done so by attaching themselves to a group of politicians. Another one-fifth of the House consisted of independent country gentlemen, ready to support the King's Government so long as this was compatible with their conscience, but averse to tying themselves up with political groups: they did not desire office, honours, or profits, but prided themselves on the disinterested and independent line they were pursuing; and they rightly claimed to be the authentic voice of the nation. In the centre of the arena stood the politicians, their orators and leaders fighting for the highest prizes of Parliamentary life. They alone could supply the façade of governments: the front benches in Parliament. But to achieve stability a Government required the active support of the Crown and the good opinion of the country. On matters about which public opinion felt strongly, its will would prevail; but with the House constituted as it was, with the electoral structure of the unreformed Parliament, and an electorate which neither thought nor voted on party lines, it is idle to assume that modern Parliamentary government was possible.

*   *   *

Lord Waldegrave, who had been Governor to the Prince of Wales 1752–6, wrote in 1758 a character sketch of him so penetrating and just that it deserves quoting almost in full.

The Prince of Wales is entering into his 21st year, and it would be unfair to decide upon his character in the early stages of life, when there is so much time for improvement.

A wise preamble; yet a long and eventful life was to change him very little. Every feature singled out by Waldegrave finds copious illustration in the fifty years that followed (in one case in a superficially inverted form).

His parts, though not excellent, will be found very tolerable, if ever they are properly exercised.

He is strictly honest, but wants that frank and open behaviour which makes honesty appear amiable. . . .

His religion is free from all hypocrisy, but is not of the most charitable sort; he has rather too much attention to the sins of his neighbour.

He has spirit, but not of the active kind; and does not want resolution, but it is mixed with too much obstinacy.

He has great command of his passions, and will seldom do wrong, except when he mistakes wrong for right; but as often as this shall happen, it will be difficult to undeceive him, because he is uncommonly indolent, and has strong prejudices.

His want of application and aversion to business would be far less dangerous, was he eager in the pursuit of pleasure; for the transition from pleasure to business is both shorter and easier than from a state of total inaction.

He has a kind of unhappiness in his temper, which, if it be not conquered before it has taken too deep a root, will be a source of frequent anxiety. Whenever he is displeased, his anger does not break out with heat and violence; but he becomes sullen and silent, and retires to his closet; not to compose his mind by study or contemplation, but merely to indulge the melancholy enjoyment of his own ill humour. Even when the fit is ended, unfavourable symptoms very frequently return, which indicate that on certain occasions his Royal Highness has too correct a memory.

Waldegrave's own endeavour was to give the Prince "true notions of common things." But these he never acquired: which is perhaps the deepest cause of his tragedy.

The defect Waldegrave dwells upon most is the Prince's "uncommon indolence," his "want of application and aversion to business." This is borne out by other evidence, best of all by the Prince's own letters to Bute:

July 1st, 1756: I will throw off that indolence which if I don't soon get the better of will be my ruin.
March 25th, 1757: "I am conscious of my own indolence . . . I do here in the most solemn manner declare, that I will throw aside this my greatest enemy. . . .
September 25th, 1758: . . . that incomprehensible indolence, inattention and heedlessness that reigns within me . . .

And he says of his good resolutions: "as many as I have made I have regularly broke"; but adds a new one: "I mean to attempt to regain the many years I have fruitlessly spent."

December 19th, 1758: . . . through the negligence, if not the wickedness of those around me in my earlier days, and since perhaps through my own indolence of temper, I have not that degree of knowledge and experience in business, one of my age might reasonably have acquir'd . . .
March 1760: . . . my natural indolence . . . has been encreas'd by a kind of indifference to the world, owing to the number of bad characters I daily see. . . .

By shifting the blame on to others, he tries to relieve the bitter consciousness of failure: which is one source of that excessive "attention to the sins of his neighbour" mentioned by Waldegrave. Indeed, George III's letters, both before and after his accession, are full of it: "the great depravity of the age," "the wickedest age that ever was seen," "a degenerate age," "probity and every other virtue absorb'd into vice, and dissipation;" etc. "An ungrateful, wicked people" and individual statesmen alike receive castigation (*in absentia*) from this very young Old Testament prophet. Pitt "is the blackest of hearts," "the most dishonourable of men," and plays "an infamous and ungrateful part;" Lord Temple, an "ungrateful arrogant and self-sufficient man;" Charles Townshend is "a man void of every quality," "the worst man that lives," "vermin;" Henry Fox, a man of "bad

character," "void of principles;" Lord Mansfield is "but half a man;" the Duke of Bedford's character "contains nothing but passion and absurdity;" etc. As for George II, the Prince felt ashamed of being his grandson. And on 23 April 1760, half a year before his accession, aged twenty-two he wrote to Bute: ". . . as to honesty, I have already lived long enough to know you are the only man who possesses that quality. . . ."

In Bute he thought he had found the tutelary spirit who would enable him to live up to his future high vocation. Here are further excerpts from the Prince's letters to him:

July 1st, 1756: My friend is . . . attack'd in the most cruel and horrid manner . . . because he is my friend . . . and because he is a friend to the bless'd liberties of his country and not to arbitary notions. . . .
By . . . your friendship . . . I have reap'd great advantage, but not the improvement I should if I had follow'd your advice. . . . I will exactly follow your advice, without which I shall inevitably sink.
March 25th, 1757: I am resolved . . . to act the man in everything, to repeat whatever I am to say with spirit and not blushing and afraid as I have hitherto . . . my conduct shall convince you that I am mortified at what I have done and that I despise myself. . . . I hope this will persuade you not to leave me when all is at stake, when nobody but you can stear me through this difficult, though glorious path.

In June 1757 Leicester House were alarmed by rumours of an alliance between the Duke of Newcastle and Henry Fox, and were ascribing fantastic schemes to the Duke of Cumberland. The Prince already saw himself compelled to meet force by force or to "yield up the Crown,"

for I would only accept it with the hopes of restoring my much beloved country to her antient state of liberty; of seeing her . . . again famous for being the residence of true piety and virtue, I say if these hopes were lost, I should with an eye of pleasure look on retiring to some uninhabited cavern as this would prevent me from seeing the sufferings of my countrymen, and the total destruction of this Monarchy. . . .

August 20th, 1758: . . . by . . . attempting with vigour to restore religion and virtue when I mount the throne this great country will probably regain her antient state of lustre.

Was this a Prince nurtured in "arbitrary notions," ambitious to make his own will prevail? or a man with a "mission," striving after naively visionary aims? No doubt, since early childhood it must have been rammed into him, especially when he was being reproved, to what high station he was born; and disparaging comparisons are said to have been drawn between him and his younger brother. He grew up with a painful consciousness of his inadequacy: "though I act wrong perhaps in most things," he wrote on one occasion. Excessive demands on a child, complete with wholesome exhortations, are fit to reduce it to a state of hebetude from which it is not easy to recover. A great deal of the pattern of George III's behaviour throughout life can be traced back to his upbringing.

He spent his young years cut off from intercourse with boys of his own age, till he himself ceased to desire it. Bubb Dodington notes in his *Diary* on 15 October 1752 that the Princess Dowager of Wales

did not observe the Prince to take very particularly to anybody about him, but to his brother Edward, and she was glad of it, for the young people of quality were so ill-educated and so vicious, that they frightened her.

And so they did him for the rest of his life. Isolation by itself would be apt to suggest to a child that there was something wrong with those he had to shun; but this he was probably told in so many words. On 18 December 1753, Dodington records another talk with the Princess:

I said, it was to be wished he could have more company. She seemed averse to the young people, from the excessive bad education they had, and from the bad examples they gave.

So the boy spent joyless years in a well-regulated nursery, the nearest approach to a concentration camp: lonely but never alone, constantly watched and discussed, never safe from the wisdom and goodness of the grown-ups; never with anyone on terms of equality, exalted yet oppressed by deferential adults. The silent, sullen anger noted by Waldegrave was natural to one who could not hit back or speak freely his mind, as a child would among children: he could merely retire, and nurture his griefs and grievances — and this again he continued through life. On 3 May 1766, during a political crisis, he wrote to Bute: "I can neither eat nor sleep, nothing pleases me but musing on my cruel situation." Nor could he, always with adults, develop self-reliance: at nineteen he dreamt of reforming the nation, but his idea of acting the man was to repeat without blushing or fear what he had to say.

For the pious works which were "to make this great nation happy" Bute's "sagacious councils" were therefore indispensable. When in December 1758 Bute expressed doubts whether he should take office in the future reign, the Prince in a panic searched his own conscience:

Perhaps it is the fear you have I shall not speak firmly enough to my Ministers, or that I shall be stagger'd if they say anything unexpected; as to the former I can with great certainty assure that they, nor no one else shall see a want of steadiness either in my manner of acting or speaking, and as to the latter, I may give fifty sort of puts off, till I have with you thoroughly consider'd what part will be proper to be taken. . . .

George III adhered to this programme. On his grandfather's death he waited to hear from Bute what "must be done." When expecting Pitt at a critical juncture: "I would wish to know what I had best say. . . ." With regard to measures or appointments: "I have put that off till I hear my Dear Friend's opinion;" "If this [is] agreeable to my D. Friend I will order it to day . . . ;" "I desire my D. Friend to consider what I have here wrote, if he is of a contrary opinion, I will with pleasure embrace it." And when in November 1762 Bute de-

clared he would retire on conclusion of
peace:

I had flattered myself [wrote the King]
when peace was once established that my
D. Friend would have assisted me in purging
out corruption . . . ; . . . now . . . the Ministry remains compos'd of the most abandon'd
men that ever had those offices; thus instead
of reformation the Ministers being vicious
this country will grow if possible worse; let
me attack the irreligious, the covetous &c. as
much as I please, that will be of no effect
. . . Ministers being of that stamp. . . .

Two years on the throne had worked little
if any change in his ideas and language;
nor did the next twenty. The same high
claims on himself, and the same incapacity
to meet real situations he was faced with:
hence his continued dependence on others.
By 1765 he saw that Bute could not help
him, by the summer of 1766 he had written off Bute altogether. In the spring of
1765 he turned to the Duke of Cumberland, the bugbear of his young years: "Dear
Uncle, the very friendly and warm part
you have taken has given me real satisfaction. . . ." And to Pitt, "the blackest of
hearts": "My friend for so the part you
have acted deserves of me. . . ." In July
1765 Cumberland formed for him the
Rockingham Administration and presided
over it a quasi-Viceroy; but a few months
later Cumberland was dead. In July 1766
Chatham formed his Administration; but
a few months later his health broke down
completely. Still George III clung to him
like a molusc (a molusc who never found
his rock). "Under a health so broken,"
wrote Chatham, "as renders at present application of mind totally impossible . . ."
After nearly two years of waiting for his
recovery, the King still wrote: "I think I
have a right to insist on your remaining in
my service." Next he clung to the ineffective Grafton who longed to be relieved of
office; and when Grafton resigned, the
King wrote to him on 27 January 1770:

My heart is so full at the thought of your
retiring from your situation that I think it

best not to say more as I know the expressing
it would give you pain.

Then came North. Totally unequal to
the difficulties of the American crisis, in
letter after letter he begged the King to let
him resign. Thus in March 1778:

Lord North cannot conceive what can induce
His Majesty, after so many proofs of Lord
North's unfitness for his situation to determine at all events to keep him at the head of
the Administration, though the almost certain
consequences of His Majesty's resolution will
be the ruin of his affairs, and though it can
not ward off for a month that arrangement
which His Majesty seems to apprehend.

But the King would not hear of it. 2 July,
1779: "no man has a right to talk of leaving me at this hour. . . ." 25 October,
1780: he expects North "will show that
zeal for which he has been conspicuous
from the hour of the Duke of Grafton's
desertion."

George III's attitude to North conformed
to the regular pattern of his behaviour. So
did also the way in which after a while
he turned against North in bitter disap-
pointment. By the '70s the King spoke dis-
paragingly of Bute and Chatham; and in
time his imagination enabled him to remember how on the day of his accession he
had given the slip to them both. A month
after Grafton had resigned, George III
wrote to him: "I . . . see anew that the
sincere regard and friendship I have for you
is properly placed. . . ." Somewhat later
his resignation changed into "desertion."
When North resigned: "I ever did and
ever shall look on you as a friend as well
as a faithful servant. . . ." But incensed
at the new situation he soon started attack-
ing North, and treated him niggardly and
unfairly over his secret-service accounts.
George III's attachment was never deep: it
was that of a drunken man to railings —
mechanical rather than emotional. Ego-
centric and rigid, stunted in feelings, unable to adjust himself to events, flustered
by sudden change, he could meet situations
only in a negative manner, clinging to men

and measures with disastrous obstinacy. But he himself mistook that defensive apparatus for courage, drive, and vigour, from which it was as far removed as anything could be. Of his own mental processes he sometimes gave discerning though embellished accounts. Thus to Bute in 1762: "I . . . am apt to despise what I am not accustom'd to. . . ." And on 2 March 1797, to the younger Pitt when criticizing the way measures were weakened in passing through Parliament:

My nature is quite different I never assent till I am convinced what is proposed is right, and then. . . . I never allow that to be destroyed by after-thoughts which on all subjects tend to weaken never to strengthen the original proposal.

In short: no after-thoughts, no reconsideration — only desperate, clinging perseverance.

Still it might be said: at least he broke through his indolence. Yes, indeed: from pathologically indolent he turned pathologically industrious — and never again could let off working; but there was little sense of values, no perspective, no detachment. There is a legend about a homunculus whose maker, not knowing what to do with him, bid him count poppy-seed in a bag. That George III was doing with his own busy self. His innumerable letters which he copied in his own hand, or the long documents transcribed by him (he never employed an amanuensis till his eyesight began to fail) contain some shrewd perceptions or remarks, evidence of "very tolerable parts if . . . properly exercised." But most of his letters merely repeat approvingly what some Minister, big or small, has suggested. "Lord A. is very right . . . ;" "General B. has acted very properly . . . ;" "the minute of Cabinet meets with my fullest concurrence . . . ;" "Nothing can more deserve my approbation than" — whatever it was. But if a basic change is suggested, his obstinacy and prejudices appear. On 15 March 1778, in a letter to Lord North, he makes an unusual and startling admission:

I will only add to put before your eyes my most inmost thoughts, that no advantage to this country nor personal danger can ever make me address myself for assistance either to Lord Chatham or any other branch of the Opposition. . . .

As a rule he would sincerely assert, perhaps with somewhat excessive ostentation, that first and foremost he considered the good of the country. When told by Bute that it would be improper for him to marry Lady Sarah Lennox, he replied: "the interest of my country ever shall be my first care, my own inclinations shall ever submit to it" (and he added: "I should wish we could next summer . . . get some account of the various Princesses in Germany" — and he settled down to "looking in the New Berlin Almanack for Princesses"). When considering withdrawal from the German war, he wrote (with a sidelong glance at the late King) about the superiority of his love "to this my native country over any private interest of my own. . . ." He was "a King of a free people;" "I rely on the hearts of my subjects, the only true support of the Crown," he wrote in November 1760. They will not desert him —

if they could be so ungrateful to me who love them beyond anything else in life, I should then I realy believe fall into the deepest melancholy which would soon deprive me of the vexations of this life.

The same note, of love for this country and trust that his subjects would therefore stand by him, continues for almost twenty years. But gradually other overtones begin to mix with it. He had become the target of virulent attacks and unjust suspicions which he deeply resented. Thus to Lord North on 7 March 1780: ". . . however I am treated I must love this country." And to the Prince of Wales on 14 August 1780:

The numberless trials and constant torments I meet with in public life, must certainly affect any man, and more poignantly me, as I have no other wish but to fulfill my various duties; the experience of now twenty years has convinced me that however long it may please the Almighty to extend my days, yet I have no reason to expect any diminution of my public anxiety; where am I therefore to turn for comfort, but into the bosom of my own family?

And he appealed to his son, the future George IV, to connect himself only with young men of respectable character, and by his example help "to restore this country to its former lustre" — the old tune once more. And in another letter:

From your childhood I have ever said that I can only try to save my country, but it must be by the co-operation of my children only that I can effect it.

In the 1780s there is a more than usually heavy crop of bitter complaints about the age by one "righteous overmuch:" "it has been my lot to reign in the most profligate age," "depravity of such times as we live in," "knavery and indolence perhaps I might add the timidity of the times. . . ." And then:

I thank Heaven my morals and course of life have but little resembled those too prevalent in the present age, and certainly of all objects in this life the one I have most at heart, is to form my children that they may be useful examples and worthy of imitation . . .

With the King's disappointments in country and son another note enters his letters. He warns the Prince —

in other countries national pride makes the inhabitants wish to paint their Princes in the most favourable light, and consequently be silent on any indiscretion; but here most persons if not concerned in laying ungrounded blame, are ready to trumpet any speck they can find out.

And he writes of the "unalterable attachment" which his Electoral subjects have shown to their Princes. When George III went mad in 1788, he wanted to go back to Hanover. Deep down there was a good deal of the Hanoverian in him.

His insanity was a form of manic-depression. The first recorded fit in March 1765 was of short duration, though there may have been a slight relapse in May; and a year later he wrote to Bute —

if I am to continue the life of agitation I have these three years, the next year there will be a Council [of] Regency to assist in that undertaking.

During the next twenty-three years he preserved his normal personality. The attack in 1788 lasted about half a year: the King was over fifty, and age rendered complete recovery more difficult. His self-control weakened and his irritability increased. He was conscious of a growing weakness. Yet there was something about him which more and more endeared him to the people. He was never popular with London society or the London mob; he was much beloved in the provinces — perhaps it was his deeper kindness, his real piety, and sincere wish to do good which evoked those feelings. These appear strikingly, for instance, in his own account of his journey to Portsmouth in 1788, and in Fanny Burney's account of his progress through Wiltshire in 1789. He was not a politician, and certainly not a statesman. But in things which he could judge without passion or preconceived ideas, there appears basic honesty and the will to do the right thing. I shall limit myself to two examples. When in 1781 a new Provost was to be appointed at Eton, George III insisted on choosing a man "whose literary tallents might make the appointment respectable . . . for Eton should not be bestowed by favour, but merit." And when in 1787 a new Lord Lieutenant had to be chosen for Ireland, the King wrote to the younger Pitt about the necessity

of looking out for the person most likely to conduct himself with temper, judgement, and an avowed resolution to avoid partiality and employ the favours he has to recommend to with the justice due to my service and to the public. . . . When I have stated this Mr. Pitt must understand that I do not lean to any particular person . . . when I state that a Lord Lieutenant should have no predilection but to advance the public good I should be ashamed to act in a contrary manner.

I have given here a picture of George III as seen in his letters, "warts and all." What I have never been able to find is the man arrogating power to himself, the ambitious schemer out to dominate, the intriguer dealing in an underhand fashion with his Ministers; in short, any evidence for the stories circulated about him by very clever and eloquent contemporaries. He had a high, indeed an exaggerated, notion of royalty but in terms of mission and duties rather than of power; and trying to live up to this idealized concept, he made unreasonable demands on himself. Setting himself unattainable standards, he could never truly come to grips with reality: which condemned him to remain immature, permanency of inner conflict precluding growth. Aware of his inadequacy, he turned to others and expected them to enable him to realize his visionary program (this appears clearest in his relations with Bute); and he bitterly reproached them in his own mind, and blamed the age in which he lived, for his own inevitable failure. The tension between his notions and reality, and the resulting frustration, account to a high degree for his irritability, his deep-seated resentments, and his suppressed anger — for situations intolerable and disastrous for himself and others; and it may have been a contributory factor in his mental breakdowns. The desire to escape from that unbearable conflict repeatedly shows itself in thoughts of abdication which must not be deemed insincere because never acted upon (men of his type cannot renounce their treadmill). He himself did not understand the nature and depth of his tragedy; still less could others. There was therefore room for the growth of an injurious legend which made that heavy-burdened man a much maligned ruler; and which has long been accepted as history.

The Independence of the Crown
and the Responsibility of Ministers

SIR LEWIS NAMIER

WILLIAM BLACKSTONE in his *Commentaries on the Laws of England* (published 1764–9) describes the King as

not only the chief, but properly the sole, magistrate of the nation; all others acting by commission from, and in due subordination to him. . . .

The passage, of which this sentence forms the kernel, is singled out for criticism by Dicey in his lectures on the *Law of the Constitution* (published 1886) as an example of Blackstone's habit

of applying old and unapplicable terms to new institutions, and especially of ascribing in words to a modern and constitutional King, the whole and perhaps more than the whole of the powers actually possessed and exercised by William the Conqueror.

Dicey goes on to say,

The language of this passage is impressive. . . . It has but one fault . . . the statements it contains are the direct opposite of the truth. The executive of England is in fact placed in the hands of a committee called the Cabinet. If there be any one person in whose single hand the power of the State is placed, that one person is not the Queen, but the chairman of the committee known as the Prime Minister. Nor can it be urged that Blackstone's description of the royal authority was a true account of the powers of the King at the time when Blackstone wrote. George the Third enjoyed far more real authority than has fallen to the share of any of his descendants. But it would be absurd to maintain that the language I have cited painted his true position.

Mark the sequence of the argument: it starts with a flat denial of Blackstone's statements, then broadens out into an account of the constitutional position in the fiftieth year of Queen Victoria's reign coupled with an admission that things may have been somewhat different in 1760, yet ends with the implied assertion that fundamentally they must have been very much the same as in 1886. To Dicey, George III was obviously "a modern and constitutional King." In reality Blackstone's definition was as exact as it could be in his time, given its being put in one single short sentence. The royal authority is not described in terms reminiscent of Stuart claims; but in terms admittedly applicable to the position of a modern Prime Minister; and still more to that of the President of the United States — which in itself is *prima facie* evidence in favour of Blackstone. For America is, in certain ways, a refrigerator in which British ideas and institutions are preserved long after they have been forgotten in this country.

In 1760 the King of Great Britain was the actual head of the Executive, as the President of the United States is today; he was expected to take an active part in Government, and, by universal agreement, had the right to choose his Ministers. This was the constitutional theory consciously held by contemporaries, and usually acted upon in practice.

What then was the nature of that con-

test which took place in the early years of George III's reign, and in which the extent of the Royal power is supposed to have been at issue? A deliberate and persistent attempt was alleged to have been made by the King to stretch his authority beyond its established limits, and the outcry was raised that the standard of prerogative had been hoisted once more in Great Britain; this was answered by countercries of oligarchical confederacies formed to enslave the Crown; and the two cries seemed to bear each other out in creating the semblance of a clash of principles. But neither charge was ever formulated in clear constitutional terms, still less was it substantiated; there, a void remained — subsequently to be filled by conceptions belonging to a later age. And I ask myself: can we find in the first ten years of George III's reign a real, fundamental difference of ideas concerning the nature and extent of the Royal power; or was the dispute a logical outcome of an inherently incongruous arrangement, aggravated by personal factors and fortuitous circumstances?

Both cries are embedded — unexplained — in Horace Walpole's *Memoirs of the Reign of King George III,* one of the most remarkable works of contemporary history, and the most important repository of accurate facts, shrewd observations, and current cant and nonsense, for the first ten years of George III's reign. The theme of prerogative runs through these memoirs, only to give place to the other cry when Walpole's friend Conway is in office and in danger of being displaced.

Prerogative became a fashionable word.
the torrent which soon carried everything in favour of prerogative
a plan had been early formed, of carrying the prerogative to very unusual heights.
The almost universal aquiescence to the favourite's influence persuaded both him and his dependents that . . . prerogative would master all opposition.

These are but a few examples of dozens that could be quoted from the *Memoirs.*

Occasionally an even more sinister turn is given to the allegations, and Walpole speaks of "a new prospect of arbitrary power," "the arbitrary measures of the Court," "the strides I had seen made towards arbitrary power," etc. Yet nowhere are these allegations explained in concrete terms.

*   *   *

In groups and when in office men frequently act out of character as though driven by an extraneous force. Almost they appear as puppets subject to a power hidden behind the circumstances; a power which uses the contradictions of a situation to pull about these puppets, or men, this way and that. And if the nature and development of the conflict with which I am concerned is to be determined, the fundamental factors of the constitutional position in 1760 must first be made clear. Inquiry into the meaning of the word "prerogative" and into the allegations of "aristocratic faction" fails to yield useful results; but there was at that time a widespread constitutional theory generally accepted by statesmen and politicians. Summed up as the Independency of the Crown, it stressed the right of the King to choose his ministers, and condemned any attempt on the part of candidates for office to force themselves upon the Crown. Let us examine, one by one, the attitude to these matters of the leading contemporary statesmen.

In the reign of George II, which we have been taught to look upon as an early conception of mid-Victorian constitutionalism, during the Cabinet crisis of April 1757 the Duke of Newcastle himself put down in a memorandum a resolution. He would not

attempt by force, in Parliament, to remove or replace ministers; or in any degree to force the King contrary to his inclinations to add any persons into his administration.

When two years later, Bute, on behalf of the Prince of Wales, inquired with Newcastle and his friends what part they would take on the death of the King, Newcastle replied that they:

wished the Prince of Wales may succeed to the crown . . . in such a situation as shall leave his opinion free and enable him to form his plans of Government with advantage,

and further that they

have nothing more at heart than . . . to prevent his being overruled or constrained by any faction or combination of men whatsoever.

The point of this declaration was aimed at the Duke of Cumberland and Henry Fox — for at that time Cumberland was expected to rely on Henry Fox as leader of a dynastic opposition at the accession of George III, and not on Newcastle and Rockingham as it in fact turned out to be.

When George III succeeded to the throne, during the war and at a time when Pitt's popularity and prestige had reached their highest point, circumstances and Pitt's refusal to serve under Bute forced the King to continue the previous administration; but when in September 1761 the first break occurred in that administration and Pitt found himself out-voted by the Whig pacifists, the Duke of Devonshire, whom Walpole describes as head of the Whig party ("No man would have disputed that pre-eminence with him") commended Newcastle for the stand he took against Pitt's City supporters.

It is very plain [what] . . . is their view . . . to induce you to retire imagining by that means to get the better more easily of Lord Bute and then take possession of the King.

And Devonshire, in his diary preserved at Chatsworth, notes having told the King that if only Bute and Newcastle united cordially, Pitt

would be of no consequence, but that if they differed he would get the better of them and take possession of His Majesty, as they had done of his grandfather, which I should be very sorry to see.

This, recorded by Devonshire himself in his private diary, constitutes a declaration in favour of the independency of the Crown which recent historians would hardly have made us expect from the head of the Whigs.

But when, a year later, the same Duke was dismissed from office and Newcastle tried to raise a hue and cry among the Whigs, Bute, in seeking to secure support for the King, alleged in circular letters that "the most factious combination of soi-disant great men had been formed against the lawful right and liberty of the King, that ever happened in this country," and that they tried to give the law to the King.

And when on 1 April 1763 Bute wrote to Grenville about a talk he had with Egremont and Halifax, he said,

They . . . entered thoroughly into the necessity of strict union, not only among yourselves, but that of the other parts of the defenders of Government, and this as the only means of supporting the King's Independency.

Newcastle rightly foresaw what the slogan of the new administration would be. He wrote to Hardwicke on 9 April 1763,

I hear that the language now given out, is, that now the Scotchman and favourite has resigned, there remains no other question but whether the King shall chuse his ministers, or suffer others to impose them upon him. I always thought that this would be the turn the new ministers would give it. . . .

Clearly both Newcastle and the ministers thought that the use of this slogan would strengthen the administration.

When in August 1763 George III appealed to Pitt to form an administration, Grenville, when asked by his colleagues what attitude they should adopt towards the King, replied,

We entered into the King's service . . . to hinder the law from being indecently and unconstitutionally given to him. We have continued in his service upon these principles; let us leave it with the same, and let us not be *complained of* as the authors of that very measure of which we have so much right *to complain,* and have sacrificed so much to prevent.

In the negotiations between the King and Pitt, the Crown was faced with the plan of a complete and united administration of Pitt's choice. Still, when taking leave from the King, he said,

Sir, the House of Commons will not force me upon Your Majesty, and I will never come into your service against your consent.

The authority for this statement might be considered, at first sight, insufficient. Walpole records having heard it from Lord Hertford, to whom the King is alleged to have told it. But there is plentiful evidence to bear it out. Thus Newcastle writes to John White on 19 June 1764, that Pitt, in a conference with Lord Lyttelton, stated "that for one he would never force himself upon the King." And Newcastle in a memorandum of a conference, of August 1764, with Monsieur Michel, the Prussian Minister, represents him saying that "Mr. Pitt talked in the usual style, that he would never come in by force; or without the King's good will. . . ." There is a good deal more evidence to that effect.

Even when the King, unwillingly, had to take back the Grenville Administration, and they felt strong enough to enforce Bute's removal from Court, George Grenville — in circular letters sent out to his friends — still repeated the old formula that they continued "to prevent any undue and unwarrantable force being put upon the Crown," and he appealed even for Bute's brother's support "for the honour and independence of the Crown." In fact the King was now between the upper and the nether millstone: those whom he had a year earlier accused of trying to give him the law, and those who claimed to have rescued him from such oppression. Indeed Charles Jenkinson, in a memorandum on relations between Bute and Grenville preserved among his MSS., records that great pains were taken to dissuade Bute from acting against the Grenville Administration, as it would have been impossible for the King to carry on his Government by the assistance alone of those who were attached to himself and that he would be thereby obliged to put himself and his Government into the hands of some of those leaders of faction who meant to give him the law.

In the course of the next two years the Grenvilles had however so far established their influence in Parliament, and had come to feel to such an extent secure, that in the words of George III, "their whole attention was confined, not to the advantage of their country but to making themselves masters of the closet. . . ." while the King made attempts (in April and May 1765) to free himself of saviours who had acquired such preponderance as practically to dictate to him in public.

Now came the turn of the wheel — "Everything comes round in this country" said Lord Rockingham to Horace Walpole on a suitable occasion. In a letter to the Duke of Cumberland, 12 June 1765, the King refers to

Those worthy men Lord Rockingham, Duke of Grafton, Newcastle, and others, for they are men who have principles and therefore cannot approve of seeing the Crown dictated to by low men. . . .

And indeed, Newcastle himself looked upon it as a great advantage that the opposition could now enter office

without being liable to the trite, common objections of forcing the Crown—coming in without the King's approbation—being not sure of the King's support etc.

And Lord Temple in February 1766 informed the King (as Grenville noted in his Diary)

that he should esteem himself happy to be the instrument to rescue the King out of the hands of those who wanted and meant to take him prisoner.

A year later the Rockingham Government collapsed under the weight of its own inefficiency. Pitt was invited by the King to form a new administration; and in their

conference on 12 July 1766 he is reported by the King to have said,

That no man was an honest man that recommended none but his own friends, as that must be to form a phalanx to disable the Crown from dismissing them when it judged it proper.

And here again, though the authority for this statement might seem open to doubts and objections, its accuracy is borne out by Pitt's pronouncements and his general attitude to parties or factions. For instance, in his letter to the King of 25 July 1766 he writes

Permit me Sir, most humbly to add that if Lord Rockingham's being *quiet* . . . depends on no other motive than Mr. Dowdeswell continuing Chancellor of the Exchequer, I must humbly advise that a resolution be finally taken that Mr. Dowdeswell . . . is not to remain in that office.

And when the negotiations about Lord Edgcumbe and Lord Bessborough were going on in November 1766, Pitt, now Lord Chatham, sent a haughty answer "that he would not suffer connections to force the King."

Such examples could be multiplied, but to what purpose? The doctrine of the Independency of the Crown — that is the right of the King to choose his ministers — was asserted over and again in the most explicit terms. Some may think, perhaps, that Horace Walpole at least — the son of the man who is (quite wrongly) reputed to have been the first modern Prime Minister in this country — did see far into the future, and held on this matter a point of view that differed from his contemporaries. But no, not even he did. When in July 1767 negotiations were on foot, between the much weakened Chatham Administration and the Rockinghams and Bedfords, with a view to broadening the administration's bottom — as it was then termed — Walpole reports having said to Conway that

There were many independent men who would not sit still and see the closet taken by storm.

And when about the same time the Duke of Richmond, discussing with Walpole the scheme of a new administration, objected to Lord Camden as "the King's man," Walpole's retort was pointed,

I asked if they expected that every man should depend on King Rockingham and nobody on King George.

* * *

Let us now look at the relations between the ministers and the King from another angle. Once he had placed them in office and if he continued to support them, their tenure was practically unlimited, unless they were overthrown by some national disaster. Such relative permanency produced, naturally enough, a form of disloyalty, innocuous yet personally galling: I have in mind the gathering of an opposition round the Prince of Wales which was based on the conflict between fathers and sons, typical in the House of Hanover, and which was bound in its turn to embitter that family conflict. Clearly, if the support of the King was sufficient to keep more or less well-chosen ministers in office, the chances of the "outs" to come in were meagre until the King's death. And yet if he dismissed his ministers without some obvious and overwhelming reasons, or without the ministers themselves giving up their offices in despair at their own incapacity to cope with a situation, he could not but give the impression of being whimsical or even arbitrary, and was certain to create enemies for himself. In fact, in the early years of George III's reign, the unsteadiness of the Parliamentary situation was aggravated by there being no Prince of Wales capable of leading an opposition to the Sovereign. And so Bute, and the legend which soon gathered round him, and the whole problem of the so-called "King's friends," became the chief disturbing elements, and endured for the first ten years of the reign. What then were the restrictions on the King's choice of ministers? In the first place they resulted from the material — its availability. When on 1 November 1760

Devonshire urged Bute to have management for Pitt as administration would be impossible without him, Bute replied,

"My Lord, I would not for the world the King should hear such language, he would not bear it for a moment."

I answered "not bear it! He must bear it. Every King must make use of human instruments to attain human ends or his affairs will go to ruin."

Furthermore, the men who could be simultaneously placed in office were to some extent already in the habit of working together or, to put it in eighteenth-century language, were grouped in factions; and the King as a rule had to accept this fact. Lastly — a very important point — the number of men fit to hold office was by no means great, which is proved, for instance, by the failure of the Newcastle-Rockingham group to form an administration in May 1765, or to carry on effectively in 1766. These failures point a significant difference between the 1760s and our own time. A great statesman requires much the same qualities today as he then did, though these qualities will, possibly, express themselves somewhat differently; but from the middling rank and the working ministers much more was then required than is now. Today, for their political work in Parliament, ministers can call on the help of a party system which efficiently eases the running of the machinery of government. Then, not even the worst corruption could have achieved anything like such easing. Equally, in the administrative work of the departments, working ministers now enjoy the support of a highly trained Civil Service. Such assistance was almost entirely lacking to the eighteenth-century minister. The junior lords at the various boards and one or two secretaries in each department (frequently themselves sitting in the House of Commons) composed between them what might be called the first-division staff, and the burden on them, and the ministers they served, was heavy indeed. I have been through the correspondence of Lord Sandwich as Secretary of State — it is preserved at Hinchinbrooke, in the Record Office, and in the Stowe Papers in the British Museum — and there is hardly a draft which is not in the handwriting of Sandwich's under-secretary, Richard Phelps, or of Sandwich himself.

It is almost inconceivable with what trifles not only the Under-Secretary but ministers and even the King had to deal personally all the while. Small wonder that the choice of ministers open to the Crown was never great.

The Leicester House Cycle

ROMNEY SEDGWICK

The principal historical achievements of Romney Sedgwick (1894–   ) have been as an editor of documents relating to eighteenth century English history. In 1931 he published, in a limited edition, a carefully annotated edition of the memoirs of Lord Hervey, and in 1952 an abbreviated version was published which was aimed at a wider public. Sedgwick's *Letters from George III to Lord Bute, 1756–1766* reveal the fears and anxieties of the young king and his reliance on the only man whom he trusted, Lord Bute. At present Sedgwick is working as one of the editors of the *History of Parliament* project which was founded by Sir Lewis Namier. The selection below is from the introduction to his *Letters from George III to Lord Bute.*

Sedgwick is a good example of the civil servant-scholar, a type more common in Britain than in the United States. He served in the Colonial Office and the Dominions Office, and in 1949 he became Assistant Under-Secretary of State of the Commonwealth Relations Office, which post he held until his retirement in 1954.

I F so much had not already been written about George III, very little would have been required by way of introduction to these letters. Their historical interest is mainly derived from their bearing on the fictions which in his case have till recently done duty for the facts. In his own time George III was accused by his opponents of attempting to subvert the system of government established by the Revolution. By subsequent historians this charge was translated into that of attempting to subvert the system of responsible government. Thus by a double distortion he has been represented as having endeavoured to imitate the Stuarts when he ought to have antici-

pated Queen Victoria. The baselessness of this story has been exposed by Professor Namier, but historical myths are no exception to the rule that to destroy a sufficiently deep-rooted delusion it is necessary to show not only its absurdity but its origin. These letters afford an opportunity for tracing the origin of the mythology that has grown up round George III.

George III was born on 24 May, O.S., 1738, at Norfolk House, St. James's Square. He was the eldest son and second child of Frederick, Prince of Wales, who at the age of thirty-one was still addicted to amusing himself by breaking people's windows at

From *Letters from George III to Lord Bute, 1756–1766*, ed. with an introduction by Romney Sedgwick (London, 1939), pp. vii–ix, xi–xiii, xv–xix, xlii–xliii. Reprinted by permission of Macmillan and Co. Ltd.

night-time, and had recently been expelled from St. James's Palace for playing a trick on his parents so successful that it had all but resulted in his wife's giving birth to her first child in a coach. Though not mentally disordered, Frederick was certainly mentally undeveloped. His life has been justly described as "such a tissue of childishness and falsehood as could only serve to show that there is nothing which mankind will not put up with where power is lodged." Like his first cousin and namesake of Prussia, of whom he seems to have been a sort of decerebrated version, he bore no resemblance to either of his parents. In fact, Poor Fred and Frederick the Great may have been variations thrown up by the crossing of their respective families with the strain of George I's wife, their common grandmother, who spent the greater part of her life in confinement for attempting to elope with an international crook.

George III's mother, Augusta of Saxe-Gotha, is described on good authority as a woman of moderate intelligence, with much natural dissimulation, a civil address, an assenting conversation, and few ideas of her own. She had no pretensions to beauty and owed her selection to the shortage of suitable Protestant princesses. According to George II, most of the other candidates had madness in their families; and, he added, "I did not think ingrafting my half-witted coxcomb upon a madwoman would mend the breed." As a eugenic experiment the marriage was not successful. Five out of nine children died in childhood or the twenties, including a daughter, the Queen of Denmark, who was dethroned and deported to Germany in circumstances recalling the fate of her great-grandmother. Of the four survivors, the Princess Royal, married to the Duke of Brunswick, had four sons of whom one was an idiot, another a half-wit, and a third blind; and two hardly less unsatisfactory daughters, of whom one was selected by George III to be the wife of her first cousin, George IV. Two younger sons, the Dukes of Cumberland and Gloucester, did little except contract marriages so unsuitable as to lead to the passing of the Royal Marriages Act. Finally, George III himself was liable to recurrent attacks of insanity, which ultimately became permanent.

As a child, George III displayed the backwardness, dullness, and apathy characteristic of mental retardation. At the age of eleven he is said to have been still unable to read. A letter written to him by his father after he had acquired this accomplishment refers to his "great fault" as being "that *nonchallance* you have, of not caring enough to please." When he was fourteen his mother described him as backward and childish for his age and as apparently caring for no one except his brother Edward, with whom he was brought up. None of his tutors was able to make any impression on him. According to the ablest of them he was not so much idle as asleep all day long. This condition persisted till he was close on eighteen, when his last governor depicts him as averse from work, indifferent to pleasure, usually in a state of total inaction, and for practical purposes still in the nursery.

*   *   *

During the eighteenth century every Prince of Wales quarrelled with the reigning monarch and went into opposition. As heir-apparent, George II co-operated in opposition with Walpole, Frederick with Pulteney, George III with the elder Pitt, and George IV with the younger Fox. These phenomena cannot be attributed, as they often have been, to some peculiarity in the House of Hanover. To go no farther than the later Stuarts, Charles II's relations with his eldest son were compared by Dryden to those of David and Absalom, and those of James II with his eldest daughter reminded Macaulay of the House of Atreus; while Anne's career as heiress-presumptive constitutes an obvious and detailed precedent for those of subsequent Princes of Wales. The peculiarity lay not in the royal family but in the political system. At all times and in all countries heirs to thrones have tended to quarrel with reigning monarchs, but only in England, between the Revolution and the first Reform Bill, have they been provided with a safe, effective, and agreeable means of expressing their resentment and securing redress for their grievances by placing themselves at the head of the opposition and embarrassing the government.

The political importance of the Prince of Wales was derived from the influence which the King, so long as most seats in the House of Commons were held in a proprietary spirit and the spoils system prevailed, was in a position to place at the disposal of his ministers. When George I came to the throne he was correctly informed that "repeated experience" had shown that

the generality of the world [are] so much in love with the advantages a King of Great Britain has to bestow, without the least exceeding the bounds of law, that 'tis wholly in your Majesty's power, by showing your favour in due time (before the elections) to one or other of them [the two parties], to give which of them you please a clear majority in all succeeding parliaments.

The difficulty of the court, to use a term which in the eighteenth century was still used synonymously with government, was not so much to secure a majority at the elections as to satisfy the demands of their supporters afterwards. In fact the atmosphere of the House of Commons was less that of a courtly parliament than of a parliamentary court. Hence the importance of the Prince of Wales, for, as Sir Robert Walpole observed:

Everybody comes to a court to get, and if they find there is nothing to be got in present, it is natural to look out for reversions. . . . Everybody who could get no ready money had rather have a bad promissory note than nothing.

In other words, with an heir-apparent in opposition and bidding against the King,

the influence of the Crown was divided against itself, and equalled on balance only the difference between the actuarial value of the King's life-interest and the successor's reversion. This difference automatically diminished as the value of the life-interest fell with the increasing age of the reigning monarch, while the political promissory notes and post-obits of the heir-apparent, issued at a discount, redeemable on accession, and taken up for capital appreciation, correspondingly improved. In such circumstances members and supporters of the government who were discontented with their share in the favours of the Crown were encouraged to "sell spot and buy futures," till their operations made it necessary to admit the chief malcontents into a coalition government. In due course a fresh block in promotion, combined with a fresh quarrel in the royal family, led to a recapitulation of the same cycle, which, three times repeated under successive heirs-apparent, terminated in the coalitions of Sunderland and Stanhope with Townshend and Walpole in 1720, of the Pelhams with Pulteney and Carteret in 1742, and of Newcastle with Pitt in 1757.

*   *   *

The return which the Prince of Wales received for his contribution to the success of the opposition was from his point of view always and necessarily unsatisfactory. His political activities could and did procure for him some valued personal concession. For undertaking to desist from opposition George II secured the withdrawal of the social sanctions imposed on him by George I; Frederick the doubling of his allowance; and George III the right to remain at Leicester House with Lord Bute. Politically, however, the Prince of Wales had nothing to gain and everything to lose by a successful opposition, the inevitable consequence of which was that his principal followers entered a government from which he was *ex officio* excluded, so that he sacrificed his position of head of a powerful party without gaining in exchange any voice in public affairs. As this gradually dawned on each successive heir-apparent, he became increasingly resentful. It was never long before the "new side of the court" became, if possible, more unpopular at Leicester House than the old. At this stage of his career George II came to regard Walpole as a "rogue" and a "rascal," who had sold him to his father's ministers; Frederick considered that his former followers had treated him "very dishonourably," "disgracefully," and "offensively;" and to George III Pitt was "the blackest of hearts," who had "given himself either up to the K —— or the D. of N —— or else he could not act the infamous and ungrateful part he now does," and should be made in the next reign to "smart" for his "ingratitude."

The uniformity of the reactions of the various Princes of Wales to standard types of situations continues to the end of the Leicester House cycle. On the accession of George II everyone expected Walpole and his colleagues to be dismissed. Walpole himself took it for granted that his day was over and only asked to be let down lightly. "I desire no share of power or business," he told Compton, the new King's favourite, "one of your white sticks or any employment of that sort is all I ask." But when it came to the point, George II was not prepared to open his reign with a political crisis. Taking the line of least resistance, he retained Walpole and the rest of the government in office, and within a few years the "rogue" and "rascal" had become his favourite minister. Thirty-three years later the whole situation was repeated. Like Walpole, Pitt is to be found assuring Bute, George III's Compton, that he asked for nothing but Bute's good offices in the new reign to "put me in some honourable bystanding office, where I have no responsibility." Like George II, George III confirmed his predecessor's ministers in office, and within a few years was addressing the "blackest of hearts" as "my Friend for so the part you have acted deserves from me," while political observers noted that there

was nothing new under the sun — or under the grandson either.

There is no reason to suppose that this cycle would not have repeated itself between 1760 and 1780 if George II had been succeeded, as in the course of nature he should have been, by a King in the fifties with a grown-up heir-apparent. As it was, owing to Frederick's premature death, the Crown skipped a generation and descended on a youth of twenty-two. To contemporary politicians the consequences were immediately apparent. Very early in the new reign Hardwicke pointed out:

There is now no *reversionary* resource. Instead of an old King and a young successor, a young healthy King and no successor in view.

There is nothing to add to this explanation of that so-called "break in the smooth development of our constitutional history" which, according to the familiar legend, was due to "the able attempt of George III to recover the powers of the Crown . . . , to make the Prime Minister a mere instrument of the royal will, and to reduce the Cabinet to a group of the 'King's servants' in fact as well as in name."

The source of this legend is to be found in the fictions to which the oppositions of the period were obliged to resort in order to justify their activities. In the eighteenth century it was established constitutional doctrine that the King had a right to choose his own ministers and that any organised attempt to prescribe to him on the point was a wicked, factious, and almost unconstitutional combination to "force" him, to "take him prisoner," and to "tyrannise over him" by "putting the dagger at his throat." The Prince of Wales and the leaders of his opposition were engaged on precisely such an undertaking. At the same time, they were unable to deny a conception of the constitution in which the Prince, as the future King, and his followers, as his ministers designate, had a reversionary interest. They solved the difficulty by resorting to the fiction that, far from being engaged in an attack on the liberty of the sovereign, they were really endeavouring to rescue him from the tyranny of an oligarchical cabal of ministers, who had taken advantage of his difficulties to reduce him to the "shadow of royalty" and to make him virtually a "prisoner on the throne." Walpole was the first leader of a Leicester House opposition to make use of this fiction, citing the straits to which Leicester House had reduced the King as evidence for the charge that the ministry were a "cabal" and were "running the nation into an aristocracy . . . so as to establish themselves and be able for the future to give laws to the King and his son and even remove them when they shall think proper;" and George II was the first Prince of Wales of his line to come to the throne full of plans for emancipating the Crown from the control of its ministers by resuming into his own hands the control of its influence and treating his ministers as "clerks, not to give advice but to receive orders." George II's ministers were similarly accused by their opponents of keeping him "prisoner, in tutelage, in slavery;" and Frederick thus justified his second opposition:

My duty to my father calls for it. One must redeem him out of those hands that have sullied the Crown and are very near to ruin all. I will endeavour it; and I hope with my friends assistance to rescue a second time the Kingdom out of wicked hands.

In due course Pulteney and Dodington, who had spent most of their political lives in trying to force themselves into office, struck up like old barrel-organs for George III's benefit the familiar tune of "recovering monarchy from the inveterate usurpation of oligarchy;" and George III, fresh from helping as Prince of Wales to reduce the royal authority so low that George II, in his own words, instead of being able to exercise his right of choosing his own ministers, was not even allowed an option in the matter, continued his unconscious parody of his grandfather's career by coming to the throne resolved to emancipate the Crown from the ministerial "tyranny an old man groaned" under. Finally, twenty-eight years later, when Carlton House had come to fill the gap left by Leicester House, Burke and the opposition of that day, with a Prince of Wales at their head, found it convenient to revert to the pose of defenders of the rights of the Crown and to accuse the ministry of establishing an "aristocratic republic."

Such slogans had no more practical significance in 1760 than in 1727 or 1788, and would have been taken no more seriously afterwards but for the use that was made of them by Burke in the most elaborate and famous of opposition fictions, the *Thoughts on the Causes of the Present Discontents*. Burke's pamphlet is concerned with the problem presented by the influence of the Crown, in which his party in 1770, unlike the Leicester House oppositions, had no reversionary interest, but which could only be got rid of at what he regarded as the prohibitive price of also getting rid of rotten boroughs. Being unable to maintain that the Crown should have an influence in the House of Commons but that the King should be deprived of any voice in its disposal, Burke cited the stock catchwords of Leicester House as evidence that the opposition were engaged in resisting a deep-laid plot, originally concocted at the court of Frederick, Prince of Wales, for emancipating the Crown from the control of its ministers by using its own "vast influence" not, as had hitherto been the practice, "in supporting the ministers of state," but in creating a party "in . . . favour of the court against the ministry." Burke's story is as fictitious as that evolved by the Leicester House politicians. His imaginary "court cabal," formed to "intercept the favour, protection and influence of the Crown in the passage to its ministers," is little more than an inversion of their equally imaginary "ministerial cabal," formed "to intercept [the King's] immediate communication with his people." No one would have been more surprised than

Burke to find that these fictions should have taken in generations of historians, engaged on the "Endless Adventure" of writing history from an inadequate knowledge of materials.

This survey of Leicester House is intended to suggest, not that eighteenth-century politics were mainly concerned with the quarrels in the royal family, but that it is misleading to discuss the influence of the Crown without also taking into account that part of it which belonged to the Prince of Wales, was known as the reversion, and was usually placed at the disposal of the opposition. In particular, its object is to show that George III's behaviour as Prince of Wales must be regarded as a typical example of the normal political life-cycle of the eighteenth-century heir-apparent; that the exceptional feature of the first twenty years of his reign was the absence, not of "responsible government," which had never existed, but of the reversionary factor; and that the legend that he attempted to destroy the system of "responsible government" is derived from a political fiction, originally invented to enable him and other heirs-apparent to close their eyes to the fact that by co-operating with the opposition they were contributing to the establishment of precisely such a system.

*   *   *

Till a few years ago it was believed that from 1760–82 there was a "break in the smooth development of our constitutional history . . . caused by the able attempt of George III to recover the powers of the Crown," etc. Professor Namier has shown that this legend is unfounded and that in reality George III carried on, to the best of his more than limited ability, the system of government which he had inherited from his predecessors. For the purpose of writing a biographical introduction to the letters now printed, it has been necessary to trace the legend to its sources. These are, first, certain stock political fictions, which were always adopted by the heirs-apparent of the period; and secondly, certain misrepresentations of incidents connected with George III's education. The former were used by Burke and the latter by Horace Walpole for the purpose of constructing theories which would justify their own political actions. At a time when the history of the period was very imperfectly known, their "literary afterthoughts" were uncritically accepted and they are still embodied in the text-books. One improvement on Horace Walpole's contribution has, indeed, been effected by historians. The evil genius of the reign remains "a Scotchman of a most disaffected family," but the name of the person so portrayed has been tacitly changed from Mansfield to Bute.

IV. THE RESPONSE TO NAMIER

Innovations of Practice Rather than Principle

RICHARD PARES

Richard Pares (1902–1958) was the son of a well-known writer on Russian history, distinguished himself as a student at Winchester and Oxford, taught at Oxford and Edinburgh, and served for many years as joint-editor of the *English Historical Review*. His first major works were studies of the West Indies in the eighteenth century, after which he turned to the general history of the reign of George III, undertaking to write the volume dealing with the period for the *Oxford History of England* series. Illness prevented him from finishing this volume, but the fruit of his work was a masterly analysis of politics entitled *King George III and the Politicians*. The selection reprinted below is from a paper presented in 1951, in which Pares presented, in briefer form, the ideas which were to be developed more fully in *King George III and the Politicians*.

GEORGE III's opinions on politics and the constitution have usually been contrasted with those of some people called "the whigs." The contrast and even the terminology are no mere invention of historians. Quite early in the reign, politicians were already reviving the terms "whig" and "tory," and using them no longer, as in 1760, to denote certain groups of men who called themselves whigs and tories, but to indicate differences of opinion between people hitherto called whigs, about the constitutional rights of the crown and their proper exercise. Whigs called other whigs by the name of tories, and "pure" whiggism was increasingly identified with a kind of anti-monarchism which may or may not have been a whig principle in earlier times but was not often expressed openly in 1760. This identification had proceeded pretty far by 1780, the date of Dunning's famous resolution;[1] and two years later, when George III made Shelburne his prime minister without consulting the cabinet, Fitzpatrick thought it natural to say, "If it is suffered, there is certainly a total end of whig principles." It was Charles Fox, above all, who treated this anti-monarchism as the main principle of the British constitution, and even as a general maxim of politics by which the conduct, for example, of French revolutionary politicians might be tried. Later developments of this classical whig theory, in which history and historians played such an important part (for the politicians them-

[1] On the night of April 6, 1780 the North ministry suffered a momentary defeat when the house of commons passed a resolution offered by John Dunning, a follower of Lord Shelburne, which stated "that the influence of the crown has increased, is increasing, and ought to be diminished."

From Richard Pares, "George III and the Politicians," in *The Historian's Business and other Essays*, ed. by R. A. and Elizabeth Humphreys (Oxford, 1961), pp. 100–123. Reprinted by permission of the Clarendon Press, Oxford. For a fuller treatment of Pares' ideas see his *King George III and the Politicians* (Oxford, 1953).

selves refreshed their zeal by historical researches into the anti-monarchist movements of the past), are so well known that there is no need to illustrate them here.

Yet it is misleading, in some respects, to speak of a conflict between George III and the "whigs" as such. Although George III was a conservative, he was not a tory; his offence against the whigs was only that of thinking that there was no important difference between them and the tories — offence enough, in the eyes of Devonshire and Newcastle, who must have considered it almost as bad as thinking there was no important difference between virtue and vice. If George III's enemies were whigs, so were almost all his allies until 1807. Moreover, his allies gave him just as much trouble as his enemies, or more: the claims of the "pure" whigs, like Rockingham, who developed a whig theory and tried to monopolize the title of whig, were no more inconvenient, in practice, than those of the "impure" whigs like Grenville and Bedford. In view of all this, George III and Bute must be considered as striving against the practices of a political class rather than the doctrines of a political party; against the politicians, rather than the whigs.

But was there any conflict at all? It has lately been suggested that George III merely "carried on, to the best of his more than limited ability, the system of government which he had inherited from his predecessors." [2] This is quite true, in one sense: George III did not innovate. In another sense, I think it less true: George III did try to restore something which possibly ought to have existed, but did not exist, when he came to the throne. He did what George II ought to have done, rather than what George II had done.

If George III only did what George II had done, why did the politicians suddenly make a fuss about it? An answer has been offered to this question: it has been suggested that the normal resource of an eighteenth-century Opposition was to cultivate

[2] A quotation from Sedgwick's introduction to *Letters from George III to Lord Bute, 1756–1766.*

the heir-apparent; that, since there was no adult heir-apparent between 1760 and 1782, the Opposition, still determined to oppose, had to find some other justification and invented, by a "literary afterthought," what came to be known as the whig theories of constitutional government. Now it is very true that Oppositions had, in the past, relied upon the heir-apparent, and that they continued, with astonishing inconsistency, to do so as late as 1812 or even later, at the same time that they were consciously trying to limit the king on the throne in the exercise of his powers. Yet I do not think this theory accounts for all the facts, or even for the most important ones. Some of the stratagems of the 1760's had certainly been invented earlier. The claims and prejudices which opposed George III may have been irrational but were genuinely, even subconsciously, felt — they have not at all the air of "literary afterthoughts;" and they were not confined to the Opposition, who might have relied on the reversionary resource. George II and George III suffered, as I have said, not only from their opponents, but even more from their own employees: from Grenville's idea of the rights of a prime minister as much as from Devonshire's idea of the rights of the nobility; in short, from nearly all politicians.

Perhaps it would be unwise to lay too much stress upon the general denunciations of the political class, with which George III's early letters to Bute abound, for neither of them knew anything of politics at first hand, and both of them were inclined to cant. In their innocence they believed that it was their task to reform the public and private morals of the politicians, and to inaugurate a new world in which a just king and minister would reward merit alone — as Bute gave Dr. Johnson a pension without any political stipulations — instead of bribing the venal and the factious. These day-dreams did not long survive the light of experience. Bute told his friend Baron Mure, "within a twelve-month I have seen so much, that I blush at my former credulity, and now know that the school of politicks and the possession of power is neither the school of friendship nor the earnest of affection." George III found himself obliged "to call in bad men to govern bad men." From that day he was living in the real world, the world of second best. It was some time before he was willingly subdued to the material in which he worked; and it is worth remembering that George III, whom the later whigs considered as the arch-corrupter, set out with a sincere distaste for the corruption which he believed to be the gravest fault of the politicians as a class.

Even in his later years he tried, perhaps harder than his adversaries, to limit the infection of public life by political patronage. As a sovereign, and as the product of a largely German upbringing, he valued professional ability, professional probity, and professional experience above the qualities which passed for political qualities in the England of his day. George II too had denounced the amateurishness of noblemen and demagogues, and tried to save the army, at least, from political jobs. George III might dislike and despise his grandfather, but took after him in this respect. He too favoured the professional element in the public service and in politics. In the days of his personal rule he showed a marked preference for advancing ex-ambassadors to be secretaries of state. He had a concern for the organization of the army as a professional service, with promotion according to seniority and merit undisturbed by political or family favouritism. He would probably have liked to keep politics out of the army altogether, though he reconciled his conscience to a casuistry by which officers who voted against the ministry in the House of Commons could be punished without actually depriving them of their commissions. He seems to have restricted the interference of politics with the higher appointments of the church and the universities; he stipulated that Regius professors should be appointed for their learning alone, and that they should actually lecture. Presumably, in the eyes

of a Newcastle or a Grenville, political *naïveté* could go no further than this.

He even favoured the professional element in politics itself. The "man of business" — the comparatively humble and assiduous politician who climbed the ladder of the "efficient" offices, step by step, stood close to the crown in politics; so close, indeed, as to be called a "King's Friend." Here, too, George III sometimes tried to create something like an organized service with promotion by merit. He once complained to North, in a fit of bad temper against the coalition ministry, of "every man brought forward into offices of business being either declaimers or owing their situation to such persons, instead of being regularly bred as in other countries in the offices where they became secretaries."

He had also to deal with the members of certain other professions — sailors, soldiers, and, above all, lawyers — who often entered the House of Commons and even the ministry with a view to professional advancement. These men were not in politics for politics' sake, but for the highest rewards of their professions, which happened to be annexed to politics. They would, perhaps, have preferred to receive those rewards by merit or seniority, and to hold them during professional, not political, good behaviour. But since that could not be, it was natural for them to attach themselves to the king, who entertained somewhat similar ideas, and represented, above all, the element of continuity in politics. They stood closer than their colleagues to the king; and it was no accident that Lord Chancellors Northington, Thurlow, and Eldon were all, in a peculiar sense, "King's Friends" — that the lord chancellor was often employed to negotiate the formation of ministries — that he sometimes tried to emphasize the professional and non-political character of his office by dissociating himself from a tottering ministry. In the eyes of the politicians, these men were rats; in those of George III, they were rather public servants who had the misfortune of being politicians. He does not seem to have shared the *n'importe-quisme* of the English, who saw nothing strange in calling a scatter-brained, horsy nobleman of tender years and untried capacity to the office of first lord of the Treasury or lord lieutenant of Ireland and replacing him, after a year or two, by another of the same kind. He did not like the dissipation of experience which these constant changes involved. I suspect that he would have been happier if politics had been an organized profession.

If George III had only complained of the politicians' amateurishness, self-seeking, and personal immorality, he would have been saying no more than many business and professional men have said from his time to ours. But there was a more precise cause of quarrel: a serious difference, of practice rather than opinion, about the exercise of the king's constitutional prerogative. It is easy to state this difference wrongly by stating it too distinctly; indeed, so indistinct is it, that some have doubted whether it existed at all. In my opinion it did exist, and I shall try to state it as carefully as I can.

The so-called "Revolution Settlement," as is well known, contained no positive statement of the king's prerogative or functions. There was a negative statement — the Declaration of Rights, which proscribed the use of particular prerogatives. This had been preceded in Charles II's reign, and was followed in those of William III and Anne, by other invasions of the crown's freedom of action — some wholly successful, such as the Mutiny Act and the new financial procedures; others wholly or partly abortive, such as the impeachment of William III's advisers on foreign policy and certain parts of the Act of Settlement.

It was possible to believe that all these things added up to something still more significant — to the principle that in a serious conflict with the House of Commons, the king must ultimately give way. Charles Fox exaggerated this idea when he asked, "Had not a majority of the House of Commons, almost from time immemorial, governed this country?" The same opinion was held in a more moderate form by Lord North, who, though he was George III's minister, was above all a House of Commons man:

Your Majesty is well apprized that, in this country, the Prince on the Throne cannot, with prudence, oppose the deliberate resolution of the House of Commons: Your Royal Predecessors (particularly King William the Third and his late Majesty) were obliged to yield to it much against their wish in more instances than one. They consented to changes in their Ministry which they disapproved because they found it necessary to sacrifice their private wishes, and even their opinions to the preservation of public order, and the prevention of those terrible mischiefs which are the natural consequences of the clashing of two branches of the Sovereign Power in the State. The concessions they made were never deemed dishonourable, but were considered as marks of their wisdom, and of their parental affection for their people.

George III neither expressly admitted nor rejected this doctrine. It was only an opinion, though perhaps a very widely held one. The visible frontier of the king's political powers was not defined by this vague opinion; it was constituted by the Declaration of Rights and the other concrete precedents. It had moved little since 1714. Within this visible frontier, the job of king was what the holder made it.

George III's three predecessors had made less of it than they could have done. Historians usually lay stress on the early Hanoverian kings' ignorance of England and the English tongue. I suspect that this is a mistake of emphasis; for George I, who suffered most from these disabilities, seems to have been the most powerful of the three because he had the strongest personality. It was Anne and, above all, George II who let the powers slip out of their hands into those of their politicians.

With Anne we are not concerned; but George II was the immediate predecessor of George III and represented everything that George III despised and eschewed. If the Princess of Wales really told her son to "be a king" — and there is no reason why she should not — it is easy to conceive her meaning: George II had not "been a king," at any rate since the death of his strong-minded wife in 1737. He spoke English; and he had an insatiable appetite for business. In Hervey's pages he is represented as stamping his foot, shouting "Puppy" or "Scoundrel," and even imagining that the decisions presented to him were really his own. That they were not; he had neither the wit to devise them nor the force of mind to insist upon them against opposition. After the death of Queen Caroline he fell into the hands of politicians — even quite minor ones, whom a strong and resourceful man could have routed. When he tried to take his decisions, the politicians combined to frustrate him and — to use the words of Carteret, one of the victims of his hesitation — the king "had not courage or activity or sufficient knowledge of the country or perhaps of mankind" to get his own way. His peevishness tried his ministers' temper; but even Newcastle, whose weak nerves could not endure the displeasure of Alderman Beckford or Mr. Hugh Valence Jones, should have known that there was no need to be afraid of his sovereign. As Hardwicke reminded him: "Your Grace owns that he does what you wish and propose, both as to English affairs and foreign affairs. That takes in the whole circle of real business." The king's reserve or ill humour therefore mattered little; and if he assumed the whole merit of measures which Newcastle had suggested to him, "For God's sake, my dear Lord, let him do so, and flatter him in it."

The politicians were soon aware of their sovereign's insignificance, just as a class of schoolboys can discern, by some occult sense, when the form-master, however noisy, does not know how to keep order. Their correspondence, their diaries, and their memoirs show a certain insouciance about the monarch. Many of their anecdotes represented him as making a fuss; very few, as getting his own way. Of

course, they could not ignore him. He occupied the central position in the constitution, even if he defended it very badly. The politicians did not so much take power from him, as use his power. When a politician wanted more power, he tried to obtain the use of it from the king. Hardwicke advised Newcastle that Pitt would be a safer partner than Fox, just because he had less influence with the king; and Pitt himself, conscious of his weakness in this respect, was reduced to "practising Lady Yarmouth" — that is, to approaching the king through the *maîtresse en titre*. But, as Carteret found to his cost in 1746 and Henry Fox in 1757, the king could not stand firm. He could say, "I shall see which is King of this Country, the Duke of Newcastle or myself," and then agree to the very condition which was, according to him, to make the Duke of Newcastle king; and all the satisfaction he got for himself was the exclusion of one or two politicians from particular offices, and the pleasure of giving Lord Hardwicke a very uncomfortable three-quarters of an hour. The ministers whom he had tried to appoint were forced to turn tail, and he had to submit to a coalition, got up by the Pelhams and their friends on the principle of buying up, at the cheapest rate obtainable, every politician who was worth buying at all. Newcastle was doubtless justified in maintaining that the unanimity thus purchased would promote the conduct of the king's business; but this excuse did not conceal from the king himself the fact that the arrangement had been made for him, not by him; that he was, as he said, "a prisoner" in the hands of "Newcastle's footmen." The politicians of the eighteenth century were perhaps too ready to believe the king a "prisoner" in the hands of the political combine who constituted the ministry of the day: volunteer rescue-parties were got up to extricate George III himself from the "shackles" of almost every minister from George Grenville to his son; but I do not see how it can be disputed that the coalition of 1757 (and, indeed, that of 1744) was negotiated by the politicians among themselves with very little regard for the king's wishes.

George III knew and despised all this. For these encroachments of the politicians upon the king's freedom to choose his ministry might very well be held to be a usurpation. Parliament, no doubt, had the right to remove a minister, by impeachment or otherwise, for criminal acts or definite failures of policy. Even this right it was expected to use in good faith, without trying to convert it from a negative to a positive power — to designate X by excluding Y. (This is why George III and his supporters demanded in 1784 that the hostile House of Commons should give the younger Pitt a fair trial unless they could allege some definite political crime against him.) Still less was parliament credited with the power of nominating the ministers.

For all that, the positive influence of the House of Commons over the composition of ministries was already greater than it looked; for the events of 1754 to 1757 had shown that the head of a government who did not sit in the House of Commons — whether he were a king or a Duke of Newcastle — could hardly hope to carry through his business without obtaining the support of at least one front-bench House of Commons politician and giving him so much power and confidence as would make him a partner rather than a hired advocate. The events of George III's reign made this clearer than ever. Even the great Earl of Chatham got into trouble from this cause. George III's personal government in the 1770's was only possible because he found in North that rarity among politicians, a House of Commons minister who was content, on the whole, to manage the House without claiming to promote himself from agent to principal; and the king had at last to capitulate to his enemies in March 1783, after the failure of a desperate search for one sizeable House of Commons figure — "Mr. Thomas Pitt or Mr. Thomas anybody" — able and willing to defend him.

This limitation, however, did not seem very formidable in 1760: George III counted on getting House of Commons ability easily enough, and it was from another quarter — from the leaders of the factions — that he expected interference with his free choice of ministers. This free choice was all-important to him; indeed, from the first political act of his reign to the last, the choice of ministers was, as it were, the vital position in the political battlefield.

At first sight this is a remarkable thing: why should so much more attention be concentrated on the king's right to choose his ministers than on his relations with them after he had chosen them? In part, for the obvious reason that if he could choose ministers whom he liked, there should be less need to define his relations with them exactly. (Cabinet procedure was extremely informal in the days of Lord North, but became ostentatiously definite and correct in 1782 and 1783, when the king and the ministers were at arm's length.) Moreover, it is far from certain that George III set out at all with the intention of interfering in detail with the daily conduct of the government. At first, in his diffidence, he merely wished to confer this power on Lord Bute, and, though he spoke of his subsequent ministers as "tools," he was still very nervous, for a time, about taking decisions. There is little evidence that he interfered much in day-to-day business until the inattention and indecisiveness of Grafton and North almost forced him, about 1768, to inaugurate a system of personal rule. In default of such a system, he could only bring his influence to bear upon policy through the choice of ministers. This, therefore, was the freedom and prerogative which he found it supremely necessary to claim; this was the symbol of the conflict between king and politicians.

George III accentuated this controversy by the use which he originally proposed to make of his power. Among the members of the "shadow-cabinet" which, like other heirs-apparent, he kept in readiness, were some men of a certain parliamentary eminence, such as Dodington and Lord George Sackville; but the chief of them, Lord Bute, had not been a member of either House since 1741. In a country governed by politicians for the last twenty years, the new king was trying to give supreme power to a man who was not a politician at all. This, I think, explains why all the politicians made a dead set at Bute. They could not have explained just why they were affronted; but affronted they were, and they let him know it. Pitt and Bute, it is evident, had long differed on the respective importance of court favour and popular eminence as titles to power. Bute, like other courtiers, thought of the court as the centre of the world, imagined that he, as the heir-apparent's representative, had made Pitt a minister in 1757, and considered as treachery Pitt's tendency to behave as if he were *sui juris*. Pitt, on the other hand, clearly thought that, though the king had a right to choose his ministers freely, yet to treat court favour as the one thing needful was, in some way, a retrogression. The Duke of Devonshire, that symbol of whig jealousy whom George III's mother not inappropriately called 'the Prince of the whigs', could not bear to see his friend Fox serve under Bute because, in effect, Bute was a nobody.

You may fancy what you please about the power of the Crown, but believe me you will find yourself mistaken. If a King of England employs those people for his ministers that the nation have a good opinion of, he will make a great figure; but if he chuses them merely through personal favour, it will never do, and he will be unhappy.

From Devonshire this doctrine filtered down to Burke, in whose *Thoughts on the Causes of the Present Discontents* it appears in denunciations of an attempt to set aside "men of talents to conciliate the people, and to engage their confidence" in favour of "men of no sort of consideration or credit in the country," and in the maxim that "Before men are put forward into the

great trusts of the state, they ought by their conduct to have obtained such a degree of estimation in their country, as may be some sort of pledge and security to the public, that they will not abuse those trusts." Burke said of Bute himself that he was a respectable man, "but who, to the moment of this vast and sudden elevation, was little known or considered in the kingdom." It is a little hard to see why these doctrines should exclude an Earl of Bute but not a Marquis of Rockingham — for how well "known or considered in the kingdom" was Rockingham when he became first lord of the Treasury in 1765, and what "pledges and security" had he given to the public? But this is one of the great mysteries of whiggery, which cannot be explained. By trying to foist Bute into the inner political circle, which considered him as a nobody because he did not already belong to it, George III began to create the belief that he was in some way disregarding the rights of his people and therefore returning to the practices of the Stuarts.

George III and Bute were not ignorant of these feelings, but expressly denied their validity; and in doing so, they were committing a slight anachronism. After all the water that had run under the bridges since 1688, it was hardly common sense, when talking of a lord chamberlain or a first lord of the Treasury, to say that it was a question whether his Majesty was to exercise the "liberty that his poorest subject enjoys, of choosing his own menial servants." George III and Bute, however, were not alone in committing this anachronism. It is pretty clear that Henry Fox agreed with them; and Henry Fox was a House of Commons man (though perhaps a disloyal one), a whig, and, in some ways, the true political heir of Sir Robert Walpole.

The Bute episode was a short one, but its consequences were important. Bute lost his nerve and resigned office in 1763, but he continued to obsess the imaginations of politicians for nearly a decade longer, above all because they believed that, though retired from active power, he continued to advise the king "behind the curtain." Their jealousy of this real or supposed secret influence aggravated the bad impression created by his original appointment, and strengthened the belief that George III claimed some right of ignoring the opinions of the parliamentary politicians. This red herring was particularly unfortunate, for George III, between 1763 and 1768, was at his most constitutional. Never again did he try to put a non-politician at the head of affairs. He had at this time no personal axe to grind, if we except his vehement desire to keep George Grenville out of his closet. Yet some of his actions in the negotiation of ministerial arrangements gave new offence to the politicians and strengthened the new "whig" theories about the way in which ministries should and should not be formed.

It is dangerous to codify too precisely George III's ideas about the formation of ministries; for, when he was fighting the politicians with their own weapons, he often had to shift his ground, and he was no more capable than his subjects — far less, for example, than George Grenville or Rockingham, and scarcely more than the elder Pitt — of seeing life steadily, in an age when politics were too much dominated by the most recent friendship and the most recent enmity. Yet his ideas, I think, can be summarized thus. The public service was, in a real sense, the king's service, and all the public servants equally and directly the king's servants. Politicians ought not to oppose that service, and even ought to enter it, when called upon to do so, without making stipulations as to policy or persons — certainly without refusing to serve with their enemies, and even, up to a point, without insisting upon bringing in their friends to serve with them (though this last, as George III knew, was usually too much to hope for, and he only once, in 1766, tried to make a point of it).

All these principles presupposed that party — "that hydra, faction" — did not or should not exist. George III, indeed, shared this opinion with many of his most respectable subjects, and there is no need to suppose that he derived it from Bolingbroke's *Patriot King*. It was natural for a young man brought up in the early 1750's to believe that there were no important differences between one clique of careerists and another, for indeed there were none. But after 1754 and, still more, after 1762, the cliques began to differentiate themselves more sharply, and even — at least in appearance — real differences of opinion began to revive within the ramshackle entity known as the whig party. The brief tenures of office in the troubled 1760's, sometimes terminated by a symbolical proscription which only an equally symbolical restitution could avenge, created swarms of claims for each available post, thus aggravating the difficulty of composing a ministry which might endure because it satisfied a commanding majority of active politicians. Moreover the German war, the Peace of Paris, the persecution of Wilkes, the Stamp Act, and the Declaratory Act were different symbolical issues upon which the groups multiplied and hardened their divisions. Nearly every stiff-necked political leader differed from nearly every other stiff-necked political leader upon at least one of these issues, and could not forget it.

In these circumstances, how could the king's service be carried on? Nobody, before Rockingham, objected on principle to an *omnium gatherum*, a "coalition of the wise and good." The Pelhams had made one in the 1740's (though this was rather a coalition of nuisance-values), and the war had brought about another in 1757. But it was becoming increasingly difficult for the wise and good to agree, at the same time that disagreement between ministers was ceasing to be thought respectable. The spectacle of Chatham's House of Commons ministers at sixes and sevens over the East India Company was thought discreditable in 1767, and that of the feebly pro-American Grafton, outvoted in his own cabinet by the anti-American Bedfords, was rightly treated by Burke as an awful warning against trying to form a ministry of the wise and good without regard to their political opinions. Even Oppositions found some difficulty, from the same causes, in opposing successfully. Differences about America did something, though differences about General Conway did much more, to prevent the formation of a Rockingham–Bedford–Grenville coalition in 1767; and one shibboleth after another kept Chatham's and Rockingham's followers apart till 1779. Above all, when a great question of policy, such as the American war or the French wars, reduced the opposites to two, the belief in an all-party coalition under the king wilted away altogether.

This, however, was a gradual process, and was not nearly completed during the crucial parliamentary sessions of 1762–6. Even in those years the behaviour of the cliques was not such as to raise George III's respect for them; for it was perfectly obvious that in 1762 Newcastle's supporters had decided to go into opposition before they knew what they were going to oppose, and denounced a peace treaty which — in most respects — they would have been only too glad to make themselves; equally obvious that both Grenville and Rockingham had taken up their attitudes on the American question almost by accident. Once, however, the attitude was taken up, it could not be abandoned. Fatigued by all their claims, George III in 1766 took part, with the elder Pitt, in an ambitious scheme for pulverizing each of these connexions. Gower was to be offered the Admiralty on condition that he came unaccompanied by his fellow-Bedfords; and when Rockingham's followers within the ministry demanded, as a body, that one of their number should retain a certain office, Chatham and the king refused all accommodation — even though it could easily have been made by a rearrangement among the Rockinghams themselves — in order to point the moral that the king and the minister would only deal with the individual, not with the group to which he belonged. They failed in both endeavours: Gower would not come alone; the Rockinghams resigned *en bloc,* thereby

repeating the traditional manœuvre of the whig malcontents, which had twice brought George II to heel and never failed to annoy George III. They did not, on this occasion, succeed in overturning Chatham's ministry, but they did destroy the last hope of an all-party coalition, and reduced Chatham to a very precarious parliamentary position. George III too suffered by his conflict with this group, whose political theory was largely founded upon its leader's long memory for injuries received and determination never to make the same mistake twice. The king got the reputation of trying "to dissolve every honourable connexion" between his subjects.

This accusation was strengthened in the 1770's, for it was widely believed that the king could not even refrain from playing off his own chosen underlings against each other. It is true that George III, who talked and wrote incessantly, could not always refrain from little asides which gave one of his ministers a hint that he did not think very well of another; nor was the favoured confidant always the person who might be regarded as the prime minister. In the decline and disintegration of North's ministry even the minister of the king's own choice found the king colloguing with very junior ministers behind his back. This was mainly the fault of North himself, who was almost a case for a psychiatrist; when the chief minister's will is paralysed, it is a virtue in the king and the junior ministers to keep the wheels of government turning round. Nevertheless, North disliked it, and his resentment probably accounts, in part, for his unexpected decision to join with Charles Fox in the anti-monarchical coalition of 1783. Moreover, if North's inability to fulfil his task of coordination was one cause of the spirit of intrigue and backbiting, diffused so widely through the services and the British and Irish governments at this time, that spirit could not fail to derive encouragement from the facility with which an ambitious sailor or a discontented politician could open a correspondence, directly or indirectly, with the king.

The relation between ministers and underlings had already, for other reasons, become a matter in dispute between the king and the politicians. George III (as has been said) considered the public service as his service, and all the public servants, after the fall of Bute, as equally his servants. The politicians, especially the Rockingham whigs, came to consider that some of the king's servants should be the masters of others — that a Rockingham or a Grenville was, as it were, a principal contractor for political power, at whose service the king should place the humbler official furniture, the "men of business" or "King's Friends." Horace Walpole satirized this view by asking "if they expected that every man should depend on King Rockingham and nobody on King George."

This idea may have derived from Sir Robert Walpole's conception of "the minister" with full power of discipline over subordinate colleagues: George III willingly gave such power to Bute and to Chatham; was it not right that he should equally give it to Rockingham? But Rockingham's insistence on the power to discipline the junior office-holders was also inspired by something more topical than that: by his fear (which Bedford shared) of that able band of humbler politicians, the Elliots, the Dysons, the Jenkinsons, whom he suspected at the same time of following Bute and keeping up a clandestine connexion with the king. Perhaps also (here again his long memory for grievances plays its part) by the misunderstandings of February 1766, when George III would not or could not force these men to obey the ministers' orders and vote for the repeal of the Stamp Act. Whatever the cause, Rockingham was already, before the end of his first ministry, demanding the dismissal of Dyson as an emblem of the identification of the king's will with that of his ministers. For the rest of his life he expressed peculiar vindictiveness against "men who are ready to support all Administrations," and the main achievement of his second ministry was the aboli-

tion of some posts which such men might hold. His follower Charles Fox, in the same tradition, seems to have thought that one House of Commons politician had a right to coalesce with another of the same kind, as he coalesced with North, but that it was discreditable for Pitt to coalesce with the Jenkinsons and Robinsons. Portland symbolized the same idea in another way, by refusing to show George III any names but those of the inner cabinet, demanding, in effect, that the king should appoint them at once, and then leave them, as ministers already in full possession of power, a free hand to fill up the subordinate offices.

This fear of the "string of Janissaries, who are always ready to strangle or dispatch" a minister "on the least signal," was not wholly irrational. Two classes of politicians — the extreme amateurs who always voted for the king's government because it was his, and the extreme professionals who always had to be on the winning side — both wanted to know if the king was really behind his ministers. George III was aware of this, and sometimes arranged with Grafton or North to show defaulters which side their bread was buttered, by calculated rudeness in the levee or the drawing-room. This was all very well, when it was preconcerted with the ministers; but what if it took the form of a demonstration, intentional or not, against them? It would encourage all the unattached politicians to oppose them. This is why Bedford, in June 1765, demanded that the king should "smile upon" his ministers and publicly "frown upon" their adversaries; the request was not childish, but highly rational, for the king's smiles betokened corn and wine and oil to the unattached politician, his frowns a long privation of those goods. This, again, is why George III ostentatiously refused, in 1783, to create any peerages upon the recommendation of the coalition ministers, that the unattached politician might know that he wished to be rescued from them — a signal so dangerous to the coalition leaders, that they seem to have thought of bribing the detested Thurlow with the Great Seal to persuade the king to change his mind.

Not only the composition of the ministry and the relations of its parts, but even the act by which it was negotiated, were the occasion of endless sparring between king and politicians. The king's first principle was, that no candidate for office was entitled to make conditions about the policy to be pursued; all that should be settled after he had accepted. The politicians themselves seem to have agreed that such conditions were indecent. The elder Pitt once admitted that it was improper to talk about *carte blanche,* "as it sounds like capitulating." Yet he proposed, almost in the same breath, that the king should agree to a programme of domestic and foreign policy, and refused to come in until these terms were accepted. George Grenville, returning triumphantly to office in May 1765 because George III could find no alternative to him, confronted his sovereign with four demands; when George III asked him, "Are these conditions, Mr. Grenville?," he repudiated the suggestion, but he admitted, a few minutes later, that they were *sine qua non.* Rockingham made no bones about his right to impose conditions: his four points, in 1782, were meant to reverse George III's American policy and reduce the royal influence in parliament. Probably the country would not have supported, in normal times, the imposition of terms upon the king; but the war-weary parliament now demanded that the struggle against America should be abandoned, and Rockingham, the only accepted leader of this resistance to George's American policy, was able to tack his own constitutional programme to the demand. In 1806 the situation was reversed: it was George III who wanted to know beforehand the ministry's proposals about army reform, and Grenville who tried to put off discussing it until the ministry should be in office. The change of position is significant: in 1783 it was

likely that the king's will would prevail in a question not covered by any previous arrangement; in 1806, more likely the cabinet's.

The politicians began to go a step further: not content with imposing, upon some occasions, a programme of policy before they would negotiate, they tried, upon other occasions, to obtain a blank commission. The king did not like to give *carte blanche* to a prime minister designate, or even to negotiate directly with him at all. He had a number of reasons for this — the fear of committing his dignity; the fear of losing control over the forces which still supported the existing ministry (for if the "rats" flocked to the side of the new minister before the negotiation was complete, the king might lose the power to break it off); perhaps, even, the fear of having a prime minister at all in the modern sense. He therefore generally preferred to have the negotiation conducted, or at least begun, by a third party — by the outgoing prime minister in 1763, by his uncle in 1765, by the lord chancellor in 1766, 1778–9, and 1782. The politicians, on the other hand, sparred for a direct negotiation. Pitt insisted upon it in 1765. Rockingham in 1767 (though not in 1765) demanded that the existing ministry should be considered at an end and that he should receive a direct mandate to make any proposals that might seem good to him. He does not seem to have insisted on this in 1779, and was persuaded to waive it in 1782. He had cause to repent of doing so, for George III took advantage of the negotiations having gone through Shelburne's hands, to treat Shelburne as joint prime minister. Profiting by this lesson, Portland obdurately insisted on a direct and unqualified mandate in 1783 and 1784. It began to be held by "pure" whigs that the king's part in forming a ministry should only in sending for a party leader and leaving the rest to him; so much so that in 1802 the Marquis of Buckingham spoke of "forming an administration in the usual way, that is, with *carte blanche* from the king."

All this sparring symbolized what came to be known as the "whig" doctrine of the relation of crown and politicians. Accustomed to the political inertia of the crown, as they were in the reign of George II, the politicians came to feel, though they could not well argue, that the crown ought to be politically inert and to farm out its power rather than exercise it; to register decisions made among themselves rather than take its own decisions; that the phrase "the king's service" was little more than a figure of speech.

Although George III's most conscious opponents were still astonishingly ready to rely upon the direct interposition of the crown's prerogative when they thought it likely to be exercised for their advantage, yet it is hard to believe that all their stratagems for limiting George III's freedom of action were merely a device for filling in time until they could look once more for the favour of an adult heir-apparent. In part, they arose out of the political warfare of the groups in the 1760's with which the king was necessarily involved; for, in seeking tactical advantages against each other, the groups incidentally obtained tactical advantages against the king, so far as he supported one group against another. In part, they were due to the ingrained prejudices of a political class, which had obtained the supreme control by sufferance and meant to keep it by right. The peculiarity of the Rockingham whigs — if they had any — consisted in little more than in grafting upon these prejudices the doctrine that party was a respectable and necessary means of ensuring the coercion of the king. The coercion itself was a thing upon which, whatever their professions, very many politicians of the 1750's — Grenville, Temple, Bedford, Newcastle, Devonshire, even Hardwicke — were perhaps unconsciously resolved. The theory of the constitution might not explicitly justify it; but the practice was to develop its own theory before long.

Infringement of Practical Realities
Rather than Legal Prescriptions

W. R. FRYER

W. R. Fryer (1917–   ) received his university education at Magdalen College, Oxford. He served in the British army from 1939–1945, and has taught at the University of Nottingham since 1947, where he is now Senior Lecturer in History. His main professional interests are eighteenth century England and the French Revolution. His efforts to rehabilitate some features of the "Whig interpretation" have aroused interest in Britain and America, and are a good illustration of the constant rethinking and revision which are essential to historical progress.

THE interpretation of the political ideas and behaviour of George III which holds the field today is that which derives from the work of the late Sir Lewis Namier and of other writers who make up what the Master of Peterhouse has called "the Namier school." It is sometimes described as a Tory interpretation. This adjective is certainly appropriate in at least one sense, for the view of these matters presented by Namier and the others involved a conscious repudiation of the conclusions earlier offered by historians who based their analysis of the subject on opinions derived from the "pure" Whig opponents of George III, and on Victorian-liberal ideas of what constitutional orthodoxy must have been a hundred years before the Victorian prime. The modern Tory interpretation of the King's ideas and conduct is, in many respects, far superior to the old Whig conception against which it reacts. This is almost too obvious to require formal admission, even by one who proposes to attempt something in the nature of a counter-reaction. The old Whig historians were obviously guilty of extreme partiality, and of anachronistic misconceptions too. The present paper embodies no intention to plead for a rehabilitation of any of the old Whig views of the subject *in extenso*.

I propose, however, to bring together a number of facts and suggestions which may indicate the existence of serious grounds for supposing that the modern Tory interpretation of the earlier part of the King's record also suffers from one-sidedness. It is meant to express the view that, when all necessary deductions are made, and all anachronisms avoided, there still remains a Whig interpretation which rests upon objective facts and serious valuation of their meaning. It is not pretended that this Whig restatement renders the Tory case completely bankrupt. But it will be argued that, even though George III was not the dark reactionary who figures under his name in the pages of Erskine May and Sir

From W. R. Fryer, "King George III: His Political Character and Conduct, 1760–1784: A New Whig Interpretation," *Renaissance and Modern Studies* (VI, 1962), pp. 68–88, 93–99. Reprinted by permission of *Renaissance and Modern Studies* and the author. In adapting this article for republication in this volume, omissions have been made which reduce the period covered to 1760–1782, and some minor verbal changes and additions have been made by the author. Verbal changes made for this volume are indicated in the text by brackets.

G. O. Trevelyan, neither was he the injured innocent who appears in the pages of Sir Lewis Namier; that George's contemporary opponents had a real case against the King, even though it was not, in some important respects, at all as strong as they wished it to be.

In undertaking this task, I would like to say that I do not think I am attempting anything in principle original. A number of distinguished English historians, in works published over the past ten years, have emphasized facts, and suggested interpretations, which indicate that they have differed seriously in opinion with Sir Lewis Namier over certain parts or aspects of the period. One of those historians, the Master of Peterhouse, has explicitly raised distinct and specific criticism against some of the methods and conclusions of "the Namier school." To a large extent, what I am doing in this essay is to quarry among the facts and ideas presented by Dr. Butterfield, by the late Richard Pares, and by Miss Betty Kemp[1] and (with grateful acknowledgments to each of these) to employ them in a general review of the King's part in the politics of this whole quarter of a century; in the process, I shall be building these facts and ideas into shapes which are, in one sense at least, very much my own, for I fully realize that no one of those distinguished scholars is in any degree responsible for the conclusions to which their writings have helped to bring me.

It must also be said that this essay makes no claim to the finality which it is so anxious to deny to the Tory interpretation of the subject. It adduces a number of facts, which, as facts, will be disputed by no one. But it attaches to them a weight and significance which, though (of course) entirely appropriate in my judgment, may perhaps seem less cogent to others. The paper therefore appeals in a proper spirit of modesty; its objects are tentative and experimental, even if its tone may appear decided.

I

The most hostile of the old Whig interpretations of the King's principles and conduct did not hesitate to suggest that George III derived his political views from circles which cherished a partiality for pre-Revolution conceptions of Kingship, and that when the King ascended the throne he brought with him a serious intention, not to abolish party distinctions (as was proclaimed), but, under this pretext, to destroy the Whig interest and clear the way for a revival of Toryism, as being the party more favourable to "high" views of the Royal prerogative. No intention to rehabilitate this aspect of the old Whig case against George III is involved in this paper. The whole subject of these accusations is mentioned here chiefly to rule them out from the beginning. There seems to be no evidence worth serious consideration to support the idea that Leicester House ever provided a home for ambitions of this sort; and, whether or not the future George III was directly influenced by Bolingbroke's famous pamphlet on the "Patriot King," at all events it seems gratuitous to associate either the pamphlet or its author with principles of a pro-absolutist character. The King himself has left on record very full and evidently unstudied illustrations of the political ideas which he cherished in adolescence and early manhood. The samples of these, presented by Sir Lewis Namier, like the larger range of evidence offered in Mr. Sedgwick's collection of the King's letters to Lord Bute, are clearly incompatible with the notion that the King grew up with any conscious animus against the constitutional order. The King's subsequent correspondence, and all his utterances of whatever kind, show just as clearly that he was marked throughout his long life by this same innocence of any dark ambitions towards the polity over which he presided.

[1] A reference to Betty Kemp, *King and Commons, 1660–1832* (London, 1959).

If we turn from the King's recorded opinions about the established constitutional order to his practical political conduct, we shall certainly find it equally innocent of disrespect for established *law* and established *legal forms*. Neither the double persecution of Wilkes, nor the long history of the efforts to tax or otherwise coerce the American colonists, provides any valid exception to this statement. The persecution of Wilkes may have been an error (in which, however, many — and they not all slavish dependents of the Court — were involved); but at all events it would be grotesque to regard it as involving a deliberate defiance of clear legal principles. In America, whatever may be thought of the constitutional issues involved, there can at least be no doubt that the authority with which the King's sympathies were identified was not the prerogative of the Crown alone, but the power of the Crown in Parliament; so that George III was able to claim that in this, as in other contingencies, he was "fighting the battles of the legislature."

We can, and indeed must, go thus far with the modern Tory interpretation. But Sir Lewis Namier and others have not been content to dispose of the baseless suppositions that George III had absolutist sympathies, or was somewhat high-handed with the law. They have gone on to make out that it is also impossible to maintain the far more cautious sort of complaint, which accused the King of traversing, not the *law*, but the then established constitutional *usages and proprieties*. The "Namier school" repudiates the view that this period witnessed an effort by the Crown to release itself from certain practical conditions and customs, which in the two preceding reigns had confined the King's political freedom more narrowly than formal law. The "school" argues, in effect, that there had hardly been any such regal confinement as the Whig historians suggested; that the apparent monopolizing of the powers of the Crown by certain politicians in the

later years of George II, and the consequent apparent relegation of the King to the position of a Venetian doge, were untypical and, moreover, misleading phenomena, encouraging Whig historians to imagine the existence of almost Victorian constitutional conditions a century before they really arose. Sir Lewis Namier has suggested that, in so far as this capture of George II by certain politicians really occurred at all, it was the product of special and temporary circumstances. We are invited to put away the notion that George II was at any stage obliged to accept a quasi-Victorian interpretation of his duties as a constitutional monarch, and consequently to put away also the thought that George III could possibly have infringed the spirit of the constitution by attempting to escape from that interpretation. Such thoughts, it is inferred, involve an anachronistic misreading of the state of constitutional usages in the mid-eighteenth century; and this misreading, in so far as it is not a gratuitous mistake, can appeal to nothing more substantial in the contemporary setting than the tendentious theorizings of the Rockingham Whigs, who persisted in an unfortunate attempt to caricature Victorian conditions before they had come into being.

As against all these unfortunate misunderstandings, the modern Tory interpretation insists that, in the absence of organized parties dominating the House of Commons, the Hanoverian Kings from 1714 to 1830 were and indeed had to be, not only in a legal fiction but in fact, the real working heads of the political system: they chose and replaced the Ministers, their choice determined also the direction which policy was to take, and the knowledge that the Ministers of their choice enjoyed their confidence provided the chief grounds upon which those Ministers enjoyed a majority in the Commons and gained success in their efforts to "chuse a Parliament." According to the "Namier school," the only real novelty which affected political conditions in 1760 and the following years was that "George III was young and had no competing heir;" so that politicians who wished, improperly, to contest the King's lawful, and necessary, part in politics could henceforward for a long period not do this in the name of loyalty to "the King of tomorrow," and were tempted to invent new fangled anti-monarchical theories to make opposition appear respectable, despite the want of a "shadow" King. George III, we are given to understand, quite properly ignored, or resisted, these ambitions. It was his opponents, not himself, who innovated. "The constitutional practice of George III differed little from that of George I or George II."

It follows from this that, if neither of the two German Kings was a mere Venetian doge, George III on his side cherished ambitions no more exorbitant than theirs. Mr. Romney Sedgwick in recent years took to task a learned publication, not only for appearing to suggest that George III favoured pre-Revolution conceptions of Kingship, but also for hinting the more modest alternative that he aspired to a political activity comparable to that of William III.

Now it is on all this part of the ground, all this which has to do with constitutional custom in the eighteenth century, that serious criticism of the modern Tory interpretation arises, and that battle is to be joined. But, before proceeding to join it, let us follow the modern Tory view of the subject into some detail in its assessment of political events in the first twenty years of the reign.

All the way through, we are presented with a consistent picture of a King who is loyal, not only to the existing law of the constitution, but just as much so to its accepted contemporary spirit and usage; of a King who, so far from being in any sense politically aggressive, is rather an almost pathetic victim of evil circumstances and of lying legend. To begin, it is implicitly denied that the preferment of the mere courtier, Lord Bute, above, and eventually to the exclusion of, the leading Ministers

of 1760, involved any constitutional impropriety, or justly involved the King in any blame for the political difficulties which it caused. After Bute's premature retirement come seven years of ministerial instability and weakness. Of these an explanation is given which, so far from invoking the sinister manipulations of a clique of nameless intriguers at Court (as Burke did), practically acquits the Court of any responsibility at all. The onus is placed upon the recalcitrance, or ineptitude, of the politicians to whom the young King successively, but vainly, transferred his confidence; and transferred it with a lack of reserve which makes him remarkable among monarchs.

Thus it is pointed out that in 1763 George Grenville assumed the place of Bute on the proposal of Bute himself and with the King's entire consent; but that Grenville himself carries the chief responsibility for the unhappy history of strained relations which ensued between King and Minister. Grenville made so much unpleasantness in his efforts to escape the odium and (as he thought) the secret intervention of his predecessor and patron, that his relations with the King were hopelessly vitiated. The obvious and much-longed-for next expedient was Pitt; but Pitt made difficult conditions, and withheld his final acceptance, until George III decided that Rockingham and Newcastle were at least better than a prolongation of the Grenville-Bedford regime. The King was then "loyal to the Rockinghams, until in January 1766 they themselves practically admitted that they could not carry on unless reinforced;" and it was Pitt, rather than the King, who was responsible for their destruction, for he persistently refused them the reinforcement, which they sought for from him in especial. In another sense, responsibility for their final downfall rests also on the Rockinghams themselves; for despite their weakness in Parliament, they flatly refused the second-best of an alliance with the party now led by Bute, which the King earnestly wished them to make. In the summer of 1766, however, Pitt finally consented to serve, though not in the framework of the Rockingham system; and reconstructed the ministry around himself, with the enthusiastic backing of the King. But Chatham's "own previous actions" had robbed him of valuable allies; and the breakdown of his health left his feeble entourage to confusion and to disintegration. The King, so far from planning to embarrass this ministry, waited patiently for the recovery of its head, and loyally supported his lieutenant Grafton in an effort to hold it together, until the retirement of the latter in 1770 inaugurated the long partnership between the King and Lord North.

If this view of the first decade of the reign be accepted, it follows that its troubles were mainly due, therefore, to the wayward nature and the tottering health of Pitt; and to the same causes must chiefly be assigned the "fatal" developments of the next ten years also; for it was Chatham's indignant repudiation, following his recovery, of his own former administration and its doings, together with his persistence in opposition for the remainder of his life, which placed and kept the government in the "incompetent" hands of North and his colleagues. The King, at least, loyally supported the North regime for many years; and he did so "with better grace than George II had supported the Pelhams."

The policy of coercion in America, with which Lord North, and, much more firmly, the King himself, became identified, was what chiefly rendered these years "fatal;" but on the King's behalf Sir Lewis insists that "of the measures which brought on the American conflict, none was of the King's making; neither George Grenville's Stamp Act, nor the Declaratory Act of the Rockinghams, nor the Townshend Duties." The most that can be said against the King in this respect, is that, after the initiatives of others had provoked the conflict, he stubbornly identified himself with what was, after all, the apparently obvious interest of England. It is as unjust to blame

him for mismanaging Imperial relations as to blame him for unconstitutional conduct at home; for in neither sphere was "responsible government" as yet possible.

Any interpretation of the intentions and activity of a man must finally at least involve a judgement of the character from which both proceed. Professor Namier in his Lecture before the Academy of Arts (1953) summed up his conclusions on the King's personality and psychology, as these are so fully revealed in the bulky Royal correspondence. The King's letters, Sir Lewis tells us, reveal no trace of a prince who contemplated for himself any ambitious or personally dominant role. "What I have never been able to find is the man arrogating power to himself, the ambitious schemer out to dominate." What does Sir Lewis find? A prince of very ordinary abilities, psychologically of impeded development; with a great notion of the duties rather than of the rights of his office, but deeply aware of his own inadequacy; a prince who accordingly exercised no powers which his predecessors had relinquished, claimed no influence not universally conceded to him, but rather clung with desperation to one adviser after another, and, so far from intriguing against his Ministers, for the most part passively adopted and repeated their ideas.

It is admitted that the King's attachment to ideas, as also to men, when once he had taken up with them, was marked by an obstinacy which was the product of terror; and that this obstinacy could produce even disastrous results. But only in this sense did he make any extraordinary impact on the politics of his time; and even these reactions were essentially defensive. His most strenuous acts of self-assertion came in his struggle against the Fox-North Coalition, and these were undertaken in justified self-defence against attempts to usurp his undoubted right, and duty, to wield the executive power. He was, in fact, neither big enough, nor bad enough, to have been the dominating and ambitious figure which legend has presented.

II

An interpretation of the King's political activity and character developed along such lines as these seems to me to be open to serious basic objections, objections which are in no way dependent upon the application of anachronistic mid-nineteenth century notions of constitutional usage to an earlier age, nor upon the uncritical adoption of estimates of the King formed by his enemies and detractors. Let us grant, as fully as possible, that there is no case whatever for presenting the King as an enemy of the constitution, as embodied in law. Let us grant that we must firmly resist any temptation to judge the King's career by standards of constitutional propriety not proper to the age in which he lived. It does not follow that Sir Lewis Namier's account of his career is an adequate one. The tame and rather pathetic figure presented to our scrutiny by Sir Lewis may indeed have been quite innocent of any intention to infringe the constitutional limits of his station, as they existed in his age. But, though not consciously seeking to do so, he may nevertheless have done so. My own judgement is that he did in fact infringe them, on several occasions and in various ways. And my misgivings about the "Namier school's" interpretation amount, shortly, to this, that it ignores or glosses over these facts, and gives us to suppose that all is satisfactorily explained, when we realize how far the monarch of that time was from liability to the conditions of Victoria, or to those dreamed of by the contemporary "monopolists in Whiggery." I wish to suggest, on the contrary, that George III repeatedly acted in a manner contrary to the constitutional duties of a monarch of his own age, and that this suggestion arises directly from admitted facts, quite independent of the prejudices of later generations, or of contemporary Whig purists.

He did so, as I shall try to argue, not indeed by breaking any law; but by ignoring certain conventions of behaviour which had every claim on his respect. Some of these conventions were imposed upon the King by sanctions grounded in objectively existent facts, which no British sovereign in that age could prudently or patriotically defy. Most of the cases which I want to discuss fall under that description.

*   *   *

Sir Lewis Namier and those who follow him seem to me to come curiously near a denial that there were any limitations of constitutional *propriety*, as opposed to limitations of *law*, for the British sovereign of the eighteenth century to infringe. Of course the "school" admits that the King's government could not be carried on without the collaboration of Parliament. But these writers seem anxious to minimize the importance which might be thought to attach to the occasions when Parliamentary opposition or recalcitrance brought Ministers and policies to naught, and to concentrate on the fact that *normally*, and for the very much greater part of the time involved, the King was, in practice as well as in law, free to choose his Ministers, and to maintain them in office during his own pleasure. They lay great emphasis on the point that the efforts of Parliamentary notables to force the King to dispense with some policy, or certain advisers, and accept others instead, were — if not always, at least almost always — condemned to failure. They insist that such efforts were condemned by opinion, as well as by facts. By opinion, in that all the parliamentarians concurred, in principle, to reprobate "formed opposition" and the coercion of the Sovereign in his lawful functions. By facts, because the "influence" of the Crown played a preponderant part in the "choosing" of the Commons, as well as a very important one in their proceedings, and because party distinctions played as yet no significant part in politics.

The situation was, in fact, according to Sir Lewis Namier, such as can be described in a sentence like this: "The executive was the King's, as truly as it is now (that) of the President in the United States." This interpretation seems to give no adequate place to the consequences of certain basic realities of the post-Revolution political system, realities which, in themselves, are questioned by no one, but which raised implications whose importance is, perhaps, still inadequately recognized. The reason for this inadequate recognition is no doubt to be found in the fact that the implications in question were not, in the normal course of eighteenth century politics, very obtrusive. But it is rash to conclude, as too many contemporary observers did and as too many subsequent students of the period have done, that because these implications were for most of the time unobtrusive, therefore they were not factors of constant importance. I wish to argue that the effect of these implications was to prescribe to the King certain objective standards of behaviour in the use of his executive prerogatives, and that these standards were applicable not only in a few rare emergencies, but regularly and continuously.

The basic realities mentioned above depend upon the admitted fact that the post-Revolution sovereigns could not carry on the government, even in peaceful times, without continuous recourse to Parliament, and that the House of Commons had the power, if it willed to exercise it, at any time to render impossible, or impotent, the policies or the advisers with which the King had identified himself.

The first and greatest implication, ignored or glossed over by too many writers both contemporary and later, is that in such conditions, there could be no stable and certain "balance" between the various branches of the polity; the "balance" so much reputed by contemporaries could have only a contingent, not a necessary, existence.

It is of course none the less true that the post-Revolution sovereigns were able to take advantage of certain favourable circumstances which allowed them, imperfectly and more or less uncertainly, to achieve a semblance of independence in the conduct of their government. Party

was weak, sometimes nearly or quite non-existent; the numerous "independent" members of the Commons could be relied on, in normal and quiet times, to display a certain disinterested forbearance towards the policies and the persons favoured by the King; finally, the conditions of society and of the representative system permitted the Court to develop the widely-ramifying resources of "influence" in order to bind a large fraction of the parliamentary personnel in some kind of allegiance to the Crown. It is no part of the intention of the present writer to question the practical importance of all this. It is sufficient to insist upon the point, which is surely undeniable, that the combined effect of all these favouring factors could never supply anything more than a precarious and unstable restoration of the balance between the King and the Commons. The King could never have any absolute assurance that a decisive negative would not be pronounced by the Commons against the Ministers and the policies with which he had identified himself. The power of the House of Commons to pronounce such a negative was armed with weapons too formidable for the post-Revolution Crown to resist.

Such a negative might be pronounced by informal, as well as by formal, means; and it might even happen that the difficulty of avoiding it, or even the fear of incurring it, would in itself be enough to drive Ministers from office, or into a sharp reversal of policy, or incline them from the beginning towards policies which they would not have chosen, had they not lived in consciousness of the need to placate the formidable body which so regularly assembled beside them. And, in any of these conjunctures, the King's "independence" in the conduct of his government incurred, to some extent, an infringement.

This was, however, not the only way in which the Royal liberty of choice was liable to interference. It might happen that the necessity to abandon one policy, or one ministerial combination, would leave the

King in practice with only one feasible alternative. In such a case, the power of the Commons to condemn would become practically identified with a power in effect to prescribe, even to dictate. Whether such a further limitation on the King's exercise of his lawful liberty of choice arose from the factious and unconstitutional machinations of "monopolists in Whiggery" matters little for our present purposes; for in the case assumed, the acts, or the anticipated acts, which really mattered would be the acts *of the House of Commons,* however arrived at; and these would be backed by its own decisive ultimate powers.

The effect of this ultimately absolute power of the Commons over the executive was, I maintain, to impose upon the King a number of constitutional prescriptions in the performance of his executive functions, over and above the limitations imposed on him by law or by ancient custom. These were imposed upon him, not because by observing them he would gratify the quaint superstitions of "the great Revolution families" and pave the way to the golden days of Victoria, but because, if he attempted to override them, the effect would at least be to damage the strength and efficiency of the government, and might involve a challenge to the reality (as opposed to the forms) of political power as it existed in his own time. Nor, to repeat what was said above, must we assume that these further limitations were merely cautions, applicable only in rare emergencies. They called for regular observance. Conduct which defied these limitations very intelligibly deserves the name of unconstitutional; and it seems to me that in this sense George III on several occasions behaved unconstitutionally.

It is open to anyone to deplore the constitutional developments which had, long before George III ascended the throne, destroyed any possibility of a real balance between King and Parliament, and imposed these further limitations upon the Crown. We can, on several grounds, sympathize deeply with Princes who found the situation unwelcome. But there is nothing whatever to be gained by obscuring the implications of these things in our own thinking.

Among the constitutional prescriptions of this sort, which George III at one time or another infringed, we must include the following. First, the King's choice of Ministers, legally free, was practically limited by the need to include men who were able, by their personal talents (aided, preferably, by their possession of a following in the Commons, or of great repute outside) to "manage" the House. Those Ministers who did not themselves sit in the Commons, moreover, had in practice to be chosen from the ranks of those Peers who enjoyed eminence and repute in their own House; and their usefulness was much enhanced in proportion to the following which they possessed in the Commons. The King, in fact, was practically bound to choose his Ministers from among the "politicians" *par excellence,* as Sir Lewis Namier calls them.

Within this circle, the King might, for many possible reasons, be unable to find a workable group of executive servants which did not in some degree leave him dissatisfied. The extreme illustrations of this kind are provided by the rather exceptional occasions when the actual or anticipated negative of the Commons upon one ministerial "system" left the King for the time being with only one practical alternative, and that an intensely unwelcome one. Thus, just as in the closing years of George II, the retirement of Newcastle in 1756 had necessitated a Royal surrender to the claims of the elder Pitt, so, in the time of George III, did the retirement of North in 1782 and that of Shelburne in 1783 respectively make inevitable, for the time being, a Rockingham-Shelburne Ministry in the one case, and a Fox-North Ministry in the other. But, short of such exigencies as these, the King might on many other occasions find himself saddled with men or measures more or less distasteful to himself, and unable, for fear of worse evils, to liberate himself.

If, in any such circumstances, the King, instead of waiting for a clear opportunity to change a ministerial system which he disliked, attempted in the meantime to counterwork the operations of his existing Ministers or to embarrass their relations, the effect would be to weaken, perhaps even to paralyze, the functioning of what was, however unwelcome to himself personally, his own administration. Such would be the case if the King appeared to prefer the counsel of "ministers behind the curtain" to that of his official advisers, or refused to grant the Ministers those promotions and dismissals which they regarded as necessary to their Parliamentary situation. The effect in either case would be to impair the Ministers' grasp of the Parliamentary majority, without necessarily at all improving the King's chances of a feasible change of system. If the King sowed dissensions among his Ministers, for example by attracting the special intimacy of some, in a manner calculated to arouse the jealousy and mistrust of others in equal or superior station, the effect, though different, might be even more unfortunate. The King's aberration would be much graver still, if he took upon himself to dismiss Ministers and to appoint others, in conditions which indicated a probability of serious resistance by a majority of the House of Commons.

Even if the King, in any of these contingencies, "got away with it," his success would not clear him of the charge of unconstitutional conduct, in the sense in which I am now using the term. Success would not in any way affect the question, for in any of these instances what the King would be attempting would be a defiance of the existing shape and logic of the constitutional situation. Political disturbance and weakness would be at once the index and the price of such activities.

III

It is time to come to the details of our case against George III. The King's action in conferring high, and finally the highest, ministerial office on Lord Bute is open to criticisms, to which Richard Pares and Herbert Butterfield have done the justice which neither Sir Lewis Namier, nor Mr. Sedgwick, was willing to concede. The promotion of Bute, a man entirely without standing as a "politician," broke through a well established, even necessary, convention; it inevitably offended and irritated all the politicians, and not merely those of the "old corps;" and its effect was to disturb political relations for years to come. Sir Lewis Namier himself cited the documents which show how it was no member of the Newcastle system, but the elder Pitt, who declared that Bute's ambition for "advancement to the management of the affairs of this country" was "not for His Majesty's service," and that "favour (was) not everything in this country. . . . Favour and honours might be allowed, but not within the walls of the Treasury." The very different and hopelessly unrealistic attitude of the new Court on the question is well illustrated by Bute's own remark, that the issue at stake was whether His Majesty should not possess "the liberty that his poorest subject enjoys, of choosing his own menial servants." As Richard Pares, surely very justly, remarked, "that was no longer a sensible thing to say about a ministerial appointment; it would have been already somewhat out of date in the reign of Charles II. . . . It was one thing to defend the King's liberty of choice; quite another thing to acquiesce in a choice which meant that Court favour alone was enough to make a Minister." [2] [It thus seems quite

[2] Mr. Steven Watson in *The Reign of George III, 1760–1815* (London, 1960) has denied the view that royal favor constituted Bute's only claim to office, pointing to Bute's political influence in Scotland and his wife's great fortune. In a long footnote (p. 83) which is not included in this volume Fryer disputes this contention, arguing that Lord Bute had acquired the means "to *become* a great politician in course of time," but this "does not prove that he was already an acceptable politician at the time when Royal favour raised him" to high office. Fryer also points out that "at the time of his sudden rise to power, Lord Bute was practically unknown to Parliament." [Editor's note]

impossible] to escape Dr. Butterfield's contention, that those who opposed the "Favourite" had a perfectly genuine constitutional issue of opposition, which cannot be brushed aside as non-existent, any more than as illegitimate.

We pass next to the period of the Grenville-Bedford ministry, when Lord Bute was accused of playing the role of "Minister behind the curtain" and when Grenville's obsessive anxiety to be rid, both of his obligations to Bute and of Bute's secret influence, created so much trouble. Without at all defending the moral implications of Grenville's conduct in taking office from Bute's hands, and then repudiating his "maker," it is clear that at this juncture no Minister, who desired to remain in office, could afford *not* to dissociate himself from so fatal an inheritance as Bute's unpopularity; and Bute's activity, or reputed activity, as "Minister behind the curtain" must have been doubly galling to Grenville. Now Namier readily admitted the undesirability of Bute's playing this part, once he had quitted public office; and Pares was willing to give George III credit for more common sense, and more respect for the constitution, than to desire such a role for Bute. It seems, however, that Bute nevertheless aspired to play this part, and that he enjoyed such contacts with the King after his resignation, that suspicions of his playing this part must inevitably have arisen. Moreover, at the time of Lord Egremont's death, Bute certainly advised the King — whether the King asked for his advice, or not — to reintroduce Pitt into the government; and, as was inevitable, Grenville bitterly resented that advice. The King can hardly escape a large share of responsibility for the troubles caused by these developments, whether he actually willed them or only permitted them.

We will next discuss the cases where, as seems undeniable, the King attempted to deal with administrations which he disliked, but could not or would not yet replace, by forming particular contacts with certain of the Ministers, to the effect of weakening or embarrassing others, or even the Ministry as a whole. Professor Pares has pointed out that, even though Burke was unjustified in supposing a general preference at Court for "weak, divided and dependent administrations," there are good grounds for thinking that the King preferred to push some administrations into this condition. He certainly gave George Grenville the impression that he was trying to play him off against the Bedfords, and drove Grenville to conclude "that the King had been taught that *division* was the art of government." Namier considered that George III honestly intended to commit himself to the Rockinghams in 1765. Pares thought rather that he never regarded Rockingham as much more than a *locum tenens* for Pitt. At all events it seems clear from the King's correspondence that he cultivated the particular intimacy of Northington and Egmont, among the Ministers of the first Rockingham government, in a way which can hardly have improved the efficiency of that sickly administration. In the second Rockingham government, he cultivated the intimacy of Shelburne and of Thurlow, and conducted a correspondence with the former, which promoted his ambitions as a joint Prime Minister in opposition to Rockingham.

Perhaps it is at this point that we ought to mention the Ministers' impression, in the time of the first Rockingham administration, that the King did less than he might have done to "discipline" those officeholders, "friends of Lord Bute," who refused support to the Ministers on the occasion of the repeal of the Stamp Act, and on subsequent occasions. It may be true, as Pares suggests, that "Rockingham probably credited the King with more power over these people than anyone possessed." It still seems hard to avoid the conclusion that the King's reaction to such recalcitrance among office-holders would have been very different had it occurred in North's time; he would have done much to find out exactly what were the limits of his power over them. [We need not go at length into the relations between the King and his Ministers during the period of Lord North's ascendancy. But the King's conduct at the point of North's final decision to resign certainly merits attention.] On the immediate eve of Lord North's retirement from what had become an untenable situation, he had occasion to write to the King a well known letter, which aptly illustrates the argument I am trying to sustain about the constitutional limitations of the King's powers. I have tried to argue that these limitations were grounded in existing political realities, regardless of anyone's likes and dislikes. The substance of all that has so far been asserted in this paper is admitted in this letter of Lord North, written before his coalition with Fox was dreamed of.

Your Majesty [wrote North] is well apprized that in this country the Prince on the throne cannot, with prudence, oppose the deliberate resolution of the House of Commons. Your Majesty has graciously and steadily supported the servants you approve, as long as they could be supported. . . . The Parliament have altered their sentiments, and as their sentiments, whether just or erroneous, must ultimately prevail, Your Majesty can lose no honour if you yield at length, as some of the most renowned and most glorious of your predecessors have done, to the opinion and wishes of the House of Commons. [He concluded] Your Majesty's goodness encourages me to submit whether it will not be for Your Majesty's welfare, and even glory, to sacrifice . . . opinions, displeasures and apprehensions to . . . the public safety.

Regarding this letter in its immediate setting, what is surely most remarkable about it, is that it should have been necessary for Lord North to write it; that, even after the division of 15th March, even after the announcement by the last seven independents hitherto loyal to the government, that they could no longer support it, the Royal recipient should have required earnest efforts, and a lecture on the principles of British politics, to convince him of the impracticability of his clinging any longer

to the Minister with whom he had so long identified himself.

The King finally accepted Lord North's resignation with what Sir Lewis Namier describes as a bad grace. To all seeming, he would have been prepared even then to struggle on longer, if the Minister had been willing to face the truly agonizing situation which must have been his, had he clung to office any longer. Does the King's behaviour at this conjuncture display anything less than a profound reluctance to accept the plainest implications of his constitutional position? . . .

IV

If, in all the matters now discussed, George III acted in a manner inconsistent with the plain implications of the constitutional situation which he inherited, these are facts which deserve their due emphasis, and a commensurate effort to account for them, not only one by one, but also in their cumulative significance. We cannot afford, in our retreat from the Whig interpretation of history, to allow ourselves to be driven from positions which were perfectly valid, and which are highly relevant to an understanding of the politics of the reign.

Sir Lewis Namier believed that "the constitutional practice of George III differed little from that of George I and George II." He asserted that George III tried to exercise no powers which his predecessors had relinquished, and claimed no influence not generally conceded to him. But, if the arguments which I have tried to enforce above have any substance, these assertions of a great historian (taken in any strict sense) must be very misleading. They must, at the best, only mean something significantly different from what they say. They must mean, not that George III was as constitutionally proper as his two predecessors, but merely that they were no more guilty of constitutional improprieties than he.

There is, however, more than that to be said. We can no doubt admit, with Richard Pares, that George II claimed, or would have liked to claim, a political latitude as great as George III. But it is, surely, a simple matter of fact that though George II claimed it, he certainly did not exercise it. It is indeed the case that he sometimes entertained "ministers behind the curtain" and distracted politics by trying to build unworkable administrations. It is also true that he successfully insisted on raising some of his personal friends to high position in 1727. But he never raised a Bute to the head of the Treasury; nor did he earn a reputation for thinking that "division was the art of government. . . ." These differences may no doubt be accounted for, in part, by reference to the inferior courage, and indeed skill, of George II. But at all events there is a difference between the records of the two monarchs in these respects; let us, at least, recognize that it exists.

The constitutional aberrations of George III can certainly be, in some measure at least, explained, and in the same process to some extent at least excused. I have already expressed the opinion, that a conviction that the King on certain occasions acted wrongly need not be in the least incompatible with a measure of sympathy for him or with doubts about the entire wisdom or goodness of his opponents. Similar conclusions could be expressed, in their proper place, of the actions and wishes of George II, where these were of like character.

So far as George III is concerned, very special allowances have to be made for the effect of his education and early environment. Baseless as the notion may be that he was reared by partisans of arbitrary rule, it is certain that those who had the chief parts in his political education, such as it was, were inspired by views of the contemporary political structure which were singularly inappropriate. Bute's views of constitutional realities were clearly ill-informed, formalistic, and naive — as his attitude towards his own claims on the Treasury would alone be enough to show. The new Court's attitude to the ruling politicians of the latter days of George II was derived almost entirely from the tendentious propaganda of disappointed or impatient men who itched to replace them. It is not surprising if the Prince's political notions were marked by oversimplified conceptions of the real value of the King's personal will in politics, and by a similarly over-simplified belief that the real cause of opposition to the King's wishes must be found, not in the inevitable implications of the legal powers already possessed by the House of Commons, but merely in the "black hearts" of politicians who betrayed their Prince.

Further large allowances ought to be made to the King on the score of difficult circumstances. When George III "panted" to obtain the Treasury for Bute, he was a very young and politically ill-educated man, in the grip of a great personal infatuation; he should have been warned off the design by the very man who was its intended beneficiary. When he intrigued behind the backs of Grenville and of Rockingham, excuses are harder to find; but at least it may be said that neither was a man likely to capture either his affection, or his admiration. His attitude towards Chatham, between 1766 and 1768, was certainly blameless, except perhaps in the sense that he expected unrealistically too much of the great man. His reluctance to acknowledge, by accepting the resignation of North, the finality of failure in America, and the necessity of an opposition invasion of the closet, does him no credit constitutionally, but it does credit to his intense if rather simple regard for the greatness of England. [On such grounds as these] extenuation can be pleaded; but it is, after all, extenuation and not defence.

v

Sir Lewis Namier's interpretation of the reign includes judgements not only on the King's activities and intentions, but also on the character which lay behind them. Here also the interpretation seems to me to be open to debate. And while this topic raises issues other than those concerned with the constitutional propriety of the King's attitude on certain occasions, and is obviously a much wider question than that, nevertheless a discussion of Sir Lewis's conclusions about the King's character may incidentally throw further light on the constitutional issues debated above.

The judgements of Sir Lewis Namier on the character of George III are no doubt as accurate, in one sense, as they are learned. In all that Sir Lewis on the positive side of the question asserted, there can be no ground for dissent from him. That the King had a mind of mediocre and unoriginal quality; that he had a great and morbid sense of his own inadequacy; that he clung to opinions, once he had admitted them, with great obstinacy, and to men, whom he regarded as his shield against some menacing feature of a hostile world, with desperate but rather mechanical attachment — all this is beyond question made out. But, besides these elements of positive description, Sir Lewis's account included denials and minimizations of other features which have often been read in the King's character. It seems to me that in this respect Sir Lewis, like other notable authorities on various subjects, is much better founded in what he asserts, than in what he denies. . . . It is difficult to resist the impression that he had always been, in some ways, a more positive character than Sir Lewis seems to allow, and that for many years . . . these more positive characteristics of his had been making a considerable contribution to politics in other ways than the expression of obstinacy and fixed ideas.

Richard Pares indicated some of the evidence which points to a rather more "positive," and indeed to a rather more traditional, view of the King's character. That the young George III was painfully lacking in self-assurance, as well as in any remarkable personal talents, is indeed certain; but he displayed from the beginning a very ambitious attitude towards the personal part of the King in politics, which indicates not only an over-enlarged sense of

duty but a certain aspiration, however timid, to an active leadership of the State. If timidity leads him to seek a vicarious gratification of this urge, by placing sole power to do good in the hands of his beloved Friend, at all events he marks off by a very broad line the ground to be occupied by himself and Lord Bute from that which he destines for the other figures in the political scene. Ministers, other than Bute, are "tools," and it hardly matters which tools are employed; politicians are assumed to be ignorant, or dishonest, or both. His view of the Royal part in politics is aspiring, partly at least because he thinks so poorly of the other participants in the game. When his dreams of greatness for Bute had to be abandoned, George III tried to find a political, though not a personal, *alter ego* in Chatham; and this dream also had to be given up. Meantime, his diffidence and lack of experience still prevented him from trying to take on himself the role for which he hoped to find supermen. But, in the fifteen years which elapsed between the collapse of Chatham and the resignation of North, he blossomed out, if only in the first place from necessity, and with a great effort of self-discipline, into a very active (though no doubt very unoriginal) director of government, of patronage, even of strategy. In the process, he developed, if only artificially, a power of hard work and a self-confidence which would in themselves have made a formidable political factor of any man who occupied the throne.

During these years he continued to display that element of contempt for the other factors in political life which was the concomitant, even probably in part the cause, of his own aspiration to leadership. Pares observed how the King, though identifying himself with the official claims of the Commons, in the affairs of Wilkes and as against the Americans, always rather looked down on the House as a "talking shop," and minimized the importance of any reverses which the government incurred there.

The active leadership which the King in those days enjoyed was, as Pares surely with justice claimed, quite unlike the role which George II had played in the days of the Pelhams; and it was also, we may add, equally unlike the part which that King had occupied in the time of Walpole. In this connection it is interesting to note that both Mr. Pares and Miss Kemp have attached some importance to evidence which suggests that George III did, indeed, regard King William as a model for his imitation.

It is certainly true that, as Professor Namier says, George III gave a loyal and unflagging support to Lord North and his administration. But to embody this claim in a context urging the King's similar loyalty to Bute and to Chatham, to Grenville and to Rockingham, is surely very misleading. For the King's loyalty to those earlier Ministers (it was, as I have tried to argue, somewhat questionable in the cases of Grenville and Rockingham) was the loyalty of a young and diffident ruler, anxious to place himself in the hands of others, who were to do for him what he was unable to do for himself. But the North system became very much the King's own. It was not merely that it provided him with a body of advisers prepared to accept responsibility for, and with the King's active aid to carry on, an American policy which the King had not invented, but now obstinately defended. In its later years, the system was very much more his own than that. It was he alone who preserved it in existence, by sheer strength of will, and kept up in it some semblance of unified activity, when North himself no longer believed in the war and had lost all power of initiative or of decision, while some of his colleagues would have liked to, and some actually did, abandon the field. If, through these years, the King clung desperately to North, it was not as he had once tried to cling to Chatham — like a mollusc to a rock — but as a combatant to his covering shield.

The King who could be, and do, all this had certainly become, or perhaps we should say revealed, a character considerably different from the estimate which Sir Lewis Namier gave us. He had revealed himself as no more a profound or an original mind than Sir Lewis represented him; perhaps not even as, at bottom, a more self-confident one. But he had shown himself a far more forceful and dominant one; as a man deserving, despite all his limitations, the description of formidable, and even, in a real sense, of ambitious.

Nothing of this bears directly upon the question, discussed above, of the constitutional correctness of some of the King's actions. So far as the period 1768–1781 is concerned, there is in any case no ground for imputing unconstitutional conduct to him. That he should, during the later years of that period, have continued to employ, in some cases against their better judgement, Ministers whose incapacity is fairly beyond question, and to identify himself as heavily as possible with a policy which proved in the end disastrous, were facts of the most unfortunate description; but, however imprudent, such a line could not, without anachronism, be described as unconstitutional. While the Ministers were prepared, however reluctantly, to accept responsibility for that policy, and could contrive, assisted of course by the influence of the Crown, to maintain their Parliamentary position, George III had every constitutional right to retain them in his service, whatever may be said of the wisdom of such a course. He had no motive to intrigue against or between them, moreover; and it is clear that, so far from doing this, he did what he could to hold them together.

There is, however, in one sense a connection between this appraisal of the King's character, judged in the light of his development and activity during that period, and the question of his constitutional improprieties at other times of his life. For, if his character was, or became, for all its limitations, as forceful and dominant as his political conduct during those years suggests; if he could propose to himself the example of William III; if he could continue to regard the other personnel of the political scene with a low opinion which enables us to measure the greatness of the interval which he placed between himself and his political setting — these are facts which at least make it less difficult to understand how the same man could, on occasions both earlier and later, reveal the essentially

aspiring cast of his nature, in proceedings which carried one or more steps further his ever-present urge to dispose of affairs untrammelled by anything less than the law. They are facts which help to explain how, despite his sincere regard for the law of the constitution, he could still misinterpret the constitution's practical contemporary meaning, and infringe its prescriptions.

The Framework of Ideas and Purposes

HERBERT BUTTERFIELD

Herbert Butterfield (1900–   ) is Master of Peterhouse and professor of modern history at Cambridge. His *The Whig Interpretation of History* examined the distortions which arise when the historian views the past from the perspective of the present, and his *George III and the Historians* reviewed historical writing on George III from Adolphus to the present, criticizing both the Whig historians of the nineteenth century and the Namier school. The article reprinted here presents, in more compact form, the arguments advanced against the Namier school in *George III and the Historians*.

I N THE *Cambridge Review* for 31 October 1930 (pp. 73–4) D. A. Winstanley — long the leading authority in the field — applauded the researches that lay behind Professor Namier's *England in the Age of the American Revolution*. Readers, he said, would now have to "consider the necessity" of revising the views they had hitherto held about the early years of George III's reign. In regard to certain incidental matters he was prepared to concede the point that "some revision" would be found to be unavoidable. "Yet," he added, "the main outlines of the story and the characters of the actors remain very much as they were before." Winstanley, in fact, could not accept Professor Namier's leading idea, that George III, far from hav-

ing a system of his own, had continued the attitude and the practices of George II, the difference between the two kings being "merely" one of "emphasis and degree." His conclusion was that, after all, we need not "feel called upon to cast all our previous conceptions into the melting pot."

The topic on which Winstanley was prepared to differ from Professor Namier — this question of an alleged change of system in 1760 — was the one which for nearly two hundred years had been the main issue in the controversy over George III. It had now provided the first occasion for applying the methods of "the structure of politics" to general narrative, an experiment which had produced a considerable disruption in the larger lines of the story.

From Herbert Butterfield, "George III and the Constitution," *History*, XLIII (1958), pp. 14–33. Reprinted by permission of the author. Since the footnotes to this article are an important part of the argument they have been included exactly as they appeared originally. For a fuller treatment of Butterfield's ideas see his *George III and the Historians* (London, 1957).

It is true that the new researches tended to reduce the story to disconnected particles, so that doubt has been thrown on the view that Professor Namier meant to provide a different framework for that piece of history with which he was concerned. But he did make some emphatic assertions; and, amongst those of his supporters who claim to stand as his interpreters, some have strongly insisted upon that more general historical revision which Winstanley was unwilling to admit. There has almost been an inclination at times to treat this version as a test of "orthodoxy" in an historian. Some, moreover, have produced later writings in which the research and the arguments seem somewhat directed to the support of the same historical revision. Nevertheless, there have been other scholars since 1930 who have evidently shared the misgivings of Winstanley; and very recently, in the new journal, *Renaissance and Modern Studies* (1957), produced by the University of Nottingham, Mr. W. R. Fryer has criticized the Namierite version of the story in greater detail.

The rejection of the view that the early policy of George III involved a change of system (and thereby provoked a constitutional issue) would entail substantial alterations in the broader framework of English political history during a considerable period. Its effect upon our map of the eighteenth century is likely to be magnified, however, by changes which are being made in other parts of the narrative of George III's reign, particularly the treatment of the Rockingham Whigs. Some misgiving has been created by the way in which the followers of the Namier method have been handling the whole problem of "party" from the very beginning of the eighteenth century. This, again, is a matter which is calculated to produce important displacements in the main lines of our general history. In all these cases there had been need for a revision of the over-simplified diagram which had provided the basis for the work of the Whig historians. And, though revision had been taking place at least from

the beginning of the twentieth century, it could be argued that this work still required to be carried further. On the other hand, while obscurantism and rigidity are always a danger, it is a matter of some moment when revisions are carried to the point at which they break down the wider framework of our general narrative.

The student of history, therefore, should have his critical faculties awake, even when he is dealing with works so scholarly, so packed with documentation, as those of Sir Lewis Namier and his followers. It is important to ask, in considering any historical technique, if there is anything in it which tends of itself to elicit a certain kind of answer (and even to produce a certain kind of history) from the documents that are used. It is useful to remember also that, even when all the apparatus of an elaborate science is present, there is still room for the insertion of subjectivity and partisanship — of something which in the present instance might even be called Tory prejudice. One might properly ask whether the historical revisions which are presented to us do not depend in part on a faulty interpretation of the eighteenth-century constitution — too rigid or too royalist a view of what Sir Lewis Namier himself calls our "mixed form of government." It is desirable that historical narrative should be broken into atoms and subjected to severe analysis; but all this has to be the prelude to its reassembly. After all the work of analysis has been done, the historian cannot really escape the necessity of surveying the whole situation with something like a statesman's eye, and even embracing a wider range of considerations altogether.

I

The classical defence of George III was based on the view that this King had rightly set out to rescue the royal authority which, under the earlier Hanoverians, had suffered too great an eclipse. It was argued that "the Whigs" — whether they were regarded as a "ministerial combination" or an "oligarchy" — had cornered the political power, and stolen a march on the rest of the country. They had taken over the prerogatives and the patronage of the Crown for their own uses; and, having captured the seat of authority, they had made their position watertight by the practice of jobbery and corruption. Since the accession of George I, therefore, the king's personal power, and his chances of having a say in matters of policy, in the work of government or in the dispensing of favour, had been reduced far more radically than the men of 1688 had ever contemplated. A king who regarded the Hanoverian succession as sufficiently established — who felt safe on the throne even without an alliance with a political party — might make it his object to alter the distribution of power, and would still not be contravening the "Revolution principles" to which his family owed their crown. George III could count on pleasing many people in the country if he reaffirmed the royal authority, and disengaged it from the fetters which the oligarchy had put upon it. For the rest, he had only to set his face against political jobbery and corruption, and proclaim his determination to have nothing to do with party distinctions. Such a programme was bound to have a popular ring; and it represented just the policy for procuring the discomfiture of "the Whigs," for it would sweep their main weapons out of their hands.

As an interpretation of the intentions of George III, this account may be right or wrong. As a diagnosis of the situation of government in 1760 it may be accurate or mistaken. At any rate, the view is not one of those which have merely been fabricated out of the speculations of later historians. The letters of people like Horace Walpole, the writings of men in court circles, the propaganda of the Bute régime, and certain things said later in parliament show that this version of the story was current amongst the people who were living at the time. They show, furthermore, that in fact this was the interpretation then put

forward by the very people who were on the side of the King. It happens to be true at the same time that this interpretation was the one which established itself in English historiography from the moment that the serious study of the subject began. It was the one which was also dominant in the higher ranges of scholarship in the early decades of the twentieth century, after the German writer, von Ruville, had staged a big attack on the "Whig" version of the story. Indeed, it had even prevailed in serious scholarship during the greater part of the intervening period; for George III seems to have been more fortunate than many people in the way in which he was treated by the historians of succeeding generations. First of all, John Adolphus and Robert Bisset, and then John Wilson Croker and Lord Stanhope, came near to turning this defence of the King into a species of orthodoxy. Even "Whig" writers, like Macaulay and Lecky, often accepted the general reasoning, or reproduced the broad framework of narrative, that have been outlined above. If they managed to turn against George III, this was as a result of the procedures they adopted at the next stage of their argument.

Even at the time of the events in question, however, it had been possible for some people — for a man like Horace Walpole, for example — to approve of George III at the beginning of his reign, and then to revise this opinion at a later date in view of what had happened in the meantime. It would appear that, by the year 1775, Walpole, perhaps for a mixture of public and private reasons, had changed his sympathies, so that in retrospect he almost reversed the ideas he had had in 1760. He came to regard George III as a king who had used the pretence of an attack on the "Whig oligarchy" as cover for an attempt to revive what was really arbitrary government. George III, he said, might talk about the abolition of party, but he merely meant to break the Whigs and establish the Tories in power — he knew that the Tories would be upholders of the prerogative.

Walpole quoted Pitt as saying that before George III had come to the throne, he himself had set out to abolish party distinctions, but not for the purpose of reviving Toryism in the way that this King was doing. And Walpole embodied these later views of his in those *Memoirs* which were to have so great an influence on the historiography of the reign, so great a part in the shaping of the "Whig" interpretation.

In any case it was possible for later historians — possible indeed for the politicians of the time — to argue that George III, emancipating himself from the "Whig oligarchy," was *ipso facto* freeing himself (or was really meaning to free himself) from any and every kind of constitutional restraint. As the Victorian age proceeded it became more difficult to sympathize even with the attack on the "Whig oligarchy," if this meant the reassertion of the authority of the monarch — a policy more strange and uncongenial to the men of 1860 than to those who had flourished a hundred years before. At its extreme, the "Whig interpretation" ceased to regard the ascendancy of the Pelhams as an objectionably oligarchical system, and assumed that what had existed down to 1760 was the modern order of things, the rule of ministries based on the party-principle. On this view, George III was actually unconstitutional in his behaviour, attempting to overthrow a regularized system of parliamentary government that had already secured recognition. The more extravagant "Whig historians" also argued that, though George III did not actually introduce the practice of corruption, he was glad to find it in existence, and prolonged its life, because it provided him with the means for establishing his personal power. From the 1860's the "Whig interpretation" in one or other of its forms was to be found even amongst the more serious and academic writers on the subject; until, in the decade before the First World War, von Ruville in Germany and Winstanley in England brought the earlier "Tory" interpretation into currency again.

II

Sir Lewis Namier and his followers have always seemed to regard themselves as reacting against the "whig interpretation," though this latter suffered still further setbacks after 1914. They ask us to believe that George III was in no sense an innovator, and that he did not set out to alter the governmental system which he inherited on his succession to the throne. In this they would appear to be conceiving themselves as vindicating George's policy; and they do not seem to realize to what a degree even most of the "Whig historians" had been prepared to sympathize with the idea of an attack on the "Whig ascendancy." They differ, in fact, from the Tories who have defended, as well as from the Whigs who have denounced, the early policy of the reign.

The "Tory" defence of George III had always had its nuances; and the break which was supposed to have occurred in 1760 had been traced to its own antecedents. Certain threads of continuity, therefore, still linked the new reign with aspects of the previous one. From the first there had been an attempt to discover the genealogy of George III's ideas, and the origin of these had been carried back to the court of George's father, Frederick, the Prince of Wales. Some of the earlier historians had made the point that George II himself had often groaned against his fetters, and had merely been less fortunate than his grandson in his attempts to throw them off. Some historians had noted that, even before 1760, the elder Pitt had objected to the continued proscription of the Tories — that he shared George's antipathy to jobbery, corruption and political connection. On the other hand, it had been signally demonstrated that, though George II might have resented certain restrictions, the royal authority had not by any means been entirely eclipsed during his reign. The talk of utter "enslavement" — if it was ever intended to be taken literally, which is very doubtful — had been, therefore, extrava-gantly polemical. Almost a century ago, W. B. Donne put forward the further suggestion that George III had been persuaded to accept an exaggerated view of the degree of subservience to which monarchy had been reduced in his grandfather's time. Some of the earlier historians had distinguished between the fields in which the royal authority had been checked before 1760, and the fields in which it had had free course, even asserting that George II had surrendered power in one region of his activity for the purpose of acquiring liberation in another. At the same time certain more recent historians, including Mr. Fryer, mentioned above, have persisted in the view that George II had been placed under real constriction by combinations of ministers.

An old era always tends to overlap into the new, and it had long been known that George III, on his accession to the throne, had proposed to carry on with the existing system for the time being. It had been realized that he had found it necessary to move with some care — to tack and trim — in view of the vested interests which his policies would be likely to affect. Even if he greatly disliked having a particular minister — the Duke of Newcastle, for example — there might be conjunctures in which he would be the one to press for the man's continuance in office. He might find it necessary on occasion to play for time, or might choose for a while to accept his present predicament rather than risk falling into something worse.

The first effect of Sir Lewis Namier's narrative — his *England in the Age of the American Revolution* — is to present the reader with a picture of extremely complex detail. But in history, as in the conduct of present-day politics, it is necessary not to lose sight of the great issues — not to be blind to the broader implications of policy. A piece of research may alter the larger lines of our map of the past by uncovering an unsuspected pivotal detail: but this does not mean that it is ever right for the student of history to lose the wood for the sake of the trees. Two powers that are allied against a common enemy may suffer from so many tensions and cross-purposes as to give the impression of subterranean hostility. The counter-movements and cross-currents are not the whole story, however; and the fact that these two powers are allies may be the directing feature of the case. When we come to the year 1760, shall we say that a change of system occurred, though we know that complications will have to be introduced into the story when we examine it in detail? Or shall we pick up the opposite end of the stick and say that there was no change of system — a course not without its dangers, even if we remember that this thesis, too, would always require to be qualified as we studied it more closely?

The answer to the decisive question depends on what George III, Bute and their collaborators had in mind, behind the chaos of contradictions, cross-purposes and tactical moves. It depends on the way they chose to present the matter to the public when opposition confronted them — the shape of the issues on which they decided to fight, decided, that is to say, to divide public opinion in governing circles or in the press. It is in the minds of the men concerned — in the continuity of their reflection and their purposes — that history acquires a coherence and cohesion, instead of presenting a mere chaos of chances and conjunctures, cross-currents and inconsistencies. The story gains meaning only through that framework of ideas and purposes within which men act even when they seem only to be responding casually to circumstances — even when they appear to contradict themselves in retreats or tactical moves. It is a matter of supreme importance, therefore, that we should use all the evidence available — even the evidence that might seem irrelevant to the "structure of politics" — in order to understand the mentality of historical personages. Without this, indeed, we cannot even distinguish which are their purely tactical utterances, and which of their actions represent strategic retreats. Those nineteenth-century historians who comprehended the broader ideas and purposes of the political actors in George III's reign — who comprehended them perhaps only in a general way and without an adequate sense of the underlying "structure of politics" — are hardly likely to have escaped serious error. But they might not be so wild, or so insidiously harmful, in their mistakes as those who give their minds to mechanics and structure, without due regard for presiding ideas and avowed public purposes; and though we may never know the last secrets of mind and motive on any specific occasion, we can often find clues to a man's general attitude.

The view that George III had no intention of altering the mode of government — in the sense that so many historians from Adolphus to Winstanley had in mind — can only be maintained by means of an argument which Sir Lewis Namier and Mr. Romney Sedgwick seem not to shrink from adopting: the argument, namely, that this King was somewhat chaotic in his intellect, and came to the throne without any framework of ideas and purposes. Yet, because they have the "Whig interpretation" so particularly in mind as the enemy, Sir Lewis Namier and those who follow him seem to set themselves up as, so to speak, the professional defenders of George III. Above all, they never cease to attack the followers of the Duke of Newcastle and the party of the Marquess of Rockingham, in whom, also, they seem determined not to recognize the existence of any serious ideas and purposes. The work of the propagandists, who wrote of the politics of the time in terms of public issues, is slurred over, and, above all, the more theoretical treatises — the writings of men like Edmund Burke who discussed ideas — are repeatedly derided, as though their polemic could have had nothing to do with the things that men were thinking about. Focussing itself so exclusively on the mechanics of political action, the Namier interpretation refuses to see any serious conflict of ideas, any serious political issues, in the events of the years

1760–3, the age of Bute. The troubles of the early years of George III's reign, says Sir Lewis Namier, were due to little things, to muddles and jealousies, and to ludicrous ironies of circumstance. Mr. Romney Sedgwick dismisses as a mere "legend" the theory of "the able attempt of George III to recover the power of the Crown." He argues that one circumstance alone is sufficient to explain the supposed "break" in the story and the troubles that occurred after 1760. This was the fact that there was now no heir-apparent capable of leading an opposition party — capable of providing such a party with a ground of hope in that he might be expected to succeed to the throne in not too distant a future.

All this means that one must slur over those passages in the documents in which George III is seen to be expressing his impatience with the ministerial system, his contempt for the "jobbery" of men like Newcastle, his dream of putting an end to corruption and his hatred of that party-edifice which had resulted in the proscription of the Tories. It means sliding heedlessly over those passages in which George III expressed his determination to escape the fate of his grandfather, George II, and his resolution to be unfettered in his choice of ministers.[1] It means, in Mr. J. Brooke's

[1] The evidence is often to be found in the works of those who apparently repudiate its significance, and the question is that of the weight which is to be attached to it as a "leakage" of mentality and as an indication of the mental context in which actions are to be judged; e.g. Newcastle to Hardwicke, 10 Aug. 1761 (Namier, *England in the Age of the American Revolution*, p. 336), where Bute is quoted as saying "that the King had a notion of not being governed, led, or to that effect, by his Minister or Ministers, as the late King had been;" George III to Bute, ?23 Oct. 1762 (R. Sedgwick, *Letters from George III to Lord Bute*, p. 150), where the Queen is reported as saying that at this time "every true lover of his King and Country ought to prepare for battle against those who would fetter their King;" George III to Bute, mid-April 1762, (*ibid.*, p. 93) "the successor I have long had in my eye to the D[uke] of N[ewcastle] is a man void of his dirty arts who will think of mine and his country's good, not of jobs;" see also my *George III, Lord North and the People*, p. 3, where George III points out that "the only difference of conduct I adopted was to put an end to those un-

The Chatham Administration, the very curious omission of just those passages which showed George III's attachment to a presiding idea — his determination (when he was forming the Chatham ministry) to break the political connections.[2] We are not even without evidence for the thesis that George III did in fact look back to an earlier period — the reign of William III, in particular — and regarded it as offering a better system of relations for the purpose of the monarchy than actually existed in his own time.[3] These later letters would in themselves be insufficient to establish the purposes of George III at the beginning of his reign. But, when put alongside the earlier evidence they do confirm the resulting picture, and they show that — as one would expect — George III did have strong ideas about the government of the country and particularly about the role of the king. Indeed, he held some of them with such consistency, that his attachment to them has been one of the reasons for regarding him as an obstinate man.

In any case, it cannot be denied that, in the circle of Bute, men wrote, from the very beginning of the new reign, on the assumption that a different type of régime was now being set on foot. Some even put it on record at an early date that the primary aim was the dislodgement of the oligarchical Whigs.[4] There are signs that George III and Bute — as well as their immediate entourage — did indeed nourish a dream, and set to work in the mood of men who intend to install a new system.[5] Some of this is further evident in the taunts of the opposition, the form of the counter-attack, and the complaints about the change of language at court. Apart from all this, there is even clear evidence that Bute and his associate Dodington did discuss with one another the issue which the older historians so often regarded as crucial: the question whether, if the King broke with Newcastle, those men who had been advanced through the Duke's control of the royal patronage would stand by their attachment to the King or their gratitude to the Duke. Nothing could provide better evidence of the feeling that the patronage of the Crown had been engrossed by the Whigs, but that perhaps it was not too late to remedy the evil. From the propaganda that was produced on behalf of the court we can learn

happy distinctions of party called Whigs and Torys"—a formula that produces wide repercussions and (when the whole context is considered) obviously does affect relations with the existing Whig system.

[2] E.g. George III to Chatham, beginning of Dec. 1766 (*Chatham Corresp.*, III, 137): "A contrary conduct would at once overturn the very end proposed at the formation of the present administration; for to rout out the present method of [parties] banding together, can only be obtained by a withstanding their [the Bedford party's] unjust demands, as well as the engaging able men, be their private connections where they will" (The word "parties" is omitted in the slightly different transcription from the Windsor MSS. in Fortescue, *Correspondence of King George III*, i. 420.)

[3] George III to Lord North, 12 Feb. 1779, Fortescue, *Correspondence of George III*, IV, 275: "this Country will never regain a proper tone unless Ministers as in the reign of King William will not mind being now and then in a Minority." The letter from Lord North to George III of March 1782 (*ibid.*, V, 394–97) clearly regards George III as needing correction in respect of the submission which a British king must make to the vote of the House of Commons, and addresses itself to the question of the precedents set by past monarchs, including William III, as though it was understood that the King was attached to the idea of losing no ground which the earlier eighteenth-century monarchs had held.

[4] See my *George III and the Historians*, pp. 43, 104, 225.
[5] Lord Shelburne, in a "Memorandum of the Events of 1762" (Fitzmaurice, *Life of Shelburne* (1875) i. 141) says that Bute had "an idea of great reformations, which all men who read the theory of things, and especially men who look up at being Ministers . . . make a great part of their conversation." In an "Autobiographical Fragment" (*ibid.*, p. 48) he says that George II "did not choose to try the experiments which his Grandson is about, nor was that time by any means ripe, I believe, for them, though Lord Granville thought otherwise." *Cf.* George III to Bute, second half of Nov. 1762 (R. Sedgwick, *op. cit.*, p. 166): "I own I had flattered myself when peace was once established that my D[ear] Friend would have assisted me in purging out corruption . . . then when we were both dead our memories would have been respected, and esteemed to the end of time;" George III to Bute, at about the same date (*ibid.* i. 167), "the hour comes which has been so long wished for by my D[ear] Friend, I mean the entering on a reformation in Government."

the issues as they were chosen for presentation to the public: the King's right to the free choice of his own ministers and confidants; the propriety of liberating the royal authority from a ministerial combination and rescuing the country from an aristocratic system; and the question of the desirability of putting an end to corruption on the one hand, proscription on the other. The *Annual Register,* seeking to tell the story impartially as a matter of contemporary history, gives the same picture of the situation. Since it shows how the men of the time envisaged the issue, its evidence is relevant to the particular problem with which we are concerned. It leans to the side of the King but it recognizes the fact that a constitutional issue has been raised between the new régime and the old. All the evidence of this kind is never to be derided or merely skipped; for the historian's narrative has at least to *account for* even the discrepant witness, and the sources on which he does not choose to rely. No matter how much factiousness lay behind the story — no matter how greatly both of the parties to the conflict may have erred in their diagnosis of their own contemporary situation — the thing which men regarded as the grand public issue is bound to be the presiding feature of the case.

III

The attempt to deny the reality of the political issues of the earlier years of George III's reign has been assisted by the adoption of too literalistic an interpretation of the rights of the king. Some later writings may have corrected the earlier emphasis on this question; but this does not seem to have affected the Namier interpretation of the opening years of the reign. In any case, one must remember that in the eighteenth century different interpretations of the constitution were in constant conflict; nor is it permissible to assume that the constitution had been finally fixed, without openings for alternative courses of development.

The Revolution of 1688 provided certain safeguards against the arbitrary use of the royal power; but, with these reservations, it was still understood that the king conducted the government and appointed the ministers. His administration could not maintain itself for long without confronting parliament, however; and if there was a sense in which he could choose any man he liked as his minister, there was a sense also in which he was bound to feel that here, as in other acts of policy, his choice was highly conditioned. Even when there were no serious conflicts to divide the country, it made a great difference in the transaction of business if the minister was a man who could work tolerably well with parliament. A technique of government and a *modus vivendi* had to be worked out, and the time might come when a man's ability to manage the house of commons would be a factor in the king's desire to have him as a minister. Striding with one foot in the Closet and one in parliament, the minister could hardly fail to realize the power which this ambiguous situation enabled him to acquire. The fact that he could claim to voice British interests against "Hanoverian" policies or advisers, and against private confidants of the king in the Closet, would give him further leverage, and provided a different source of tension. A minister might argue — as Townshend and Walpole argued in 1717 — that a given policy, which the king desired, would not be acceptable to the house of commons. He might do this when he personally disagreed with the policy and was prepared to assist or even incite the parliamentary opposition that he was pretending to prognosticate.

In the face of parliament ministers could insist on the royal favour which had brought them to office and which kept them in power. They could fall back on the will of the king, which was identified with their policy, so that opposition to their decisions appeared as hostility to the king. In the face of the monarch himself, however, the same men could assert the need to placate the house of commons — they could refuse to accept responsibility in parliament for a policy of which they did not approve. Sir Lewis Namier and those who accept his interpretation, are inclined to measure the whole situation by taking the ministers — the Duke of Newcastle and others — at their word in the former of these modes of argument, while treating the latter mode as merely tactical and insincere.[6] But if

[6] E.g. *England in the Age of the American Revolution*, p. 401. In the *Sunday Times*, 8 Feb. 1953, Sir Lewis Namier compares C. J. Fox's denial of the King's right to choose his ministers with his eagerness to be appointed by George III's heir, whether as Regent or King. I think that many historians have long agreed with him that this makes the conduct of the Rockinghamites "less impressive" and indeed more factious. Too often, however, there is the innuendo that, e.g., Fox would be sincere in the latter case (which represented his real or realist policy) but not in the former case which was mere "programme"—the easy utopianism of ineffectual opposition. It must be remembered that when men, parties and even churches feel that they are in the right and that they ought to be in power, they are ready (as both Catholics and Protestants once were) to accept or seek power at the hands of the monarch without really believing that the monarch had the right to decide, the right to give the power to the other party. And, though Fox certainly was factious, the argument would apply *a fortiori* in a case such as the one quoted, when the real alternative to his holding power at the will of a Regent was his enemies holding power at the will of a King, this system being in operation whether he liked it or not. Fox addressed himself to the same fundamental issue in connection with the parallel case of corruption when it was argued that those out of power opposed corruption while those in power supported its continuance. On 8 Feb. 1780 he called for "the judgment of Solomon"—let the world see who really was prepared to vote for the abolition of this disowned child, corruption. I do not feel that the Rockinghamites came quite satisfactorily out of the test (from a twentieth-century point of view) though they did set out to trim corruption when they came into office in 1782. However, as Professor Pares points out (*King George III and the Politicians*, p. 90), Burke in 1770 claimed (and George III's complaint to a certain degree confirmed the claim) that the Rockinghamites in office had held to the principles they had adopted in opposition. Too much could be made of this, but the emergence of this point as a criterion is itself not without significance. I long ago wrote (*George III, Lord North and the People*, p. 41) that "not Rockingham or North or Fox or Grafton served England so faithfully, so nearly without a glance at private purposes or party aggrandisement" as George III; but he was obstinately self-righteous and it can hardly be denied that the opposition to him led to the development of constitutional ideas.

men were merely tactical — were merely reflecting the effect of their situation — in the one case, the same might just as well be true of the other. The remarks are to be construed, not in a literalistic manner, but always with reference to the posture or the platform from which they were delivered. In other words, the historian must penetrate behind them, range over a wider field of evidence, and carry the analysis deeper in his search for the truth.

The supposed right of the king to choose any man as his minister requires to be treated with elasticity of mind. Those who were ministers and those who were only would-be ministers might certainly compete with one another for the royal favour. When this aspect of the matter is considered, the power of the king clearly appears as an important factor in the story. On the other hand, the politicians were able to combine, and they could use the influence that was at their disposal in order to secure strength of their own in the house of commons. They might swear that the king had the right to choose his own ministers — might indeed insist that he do the choosing; but the words might sound like a taunt if they had produced a situation in which it would be catastrophic for him to choose anybody but them. He might be formally free to choose, but they could not be prevented from having a part in the establishment of that network of conditioning circumstances which always constricted his choice. And when he had chosen them, it was natural that they should stress the fact that he had selected them, and should insist on his right of choice.

Though it is true, perhaps, in a formal sense, once again it is not absolutely true that opposition to the ministry in the eighteenth century meant opposition to the king. Those who were out of office might form an opposition-party, and, as Croker explained over a century ago, might assemble themselves around the Prince of Wales, and might have faith that at least they would achieve their advancement when he came to the throne. That faith was itself a pre-

carious one, as the eighteenth century was
to show on more than one occasion. Nor is
it plausible to argue that under the Hanoverians a man in opposition could never
hope to recover favour during the lifetime
of the reigning king. This factor in the
story has been exaggerated, though it had
some significance when George II lived
longer than was expected and cheated some
men's calculations. It is not at all clear that
when a Walpole or a Hardwicke, a Newcastle or a Rockingham, went into opposition they despaired of making themselves
acceptable again — or perhaps indispensable — to the existing king.

On the other hand, when a minister lost
his office, there was a considerable likeli-
hood that he would go into regular opposition. He would not confess that he opposed
the government merely because he was not
a member of it, and in this sense we find
him constantly taking care to deprecate
"regular opposition." He would discover
that Walpole (for example) ought to be
opposed because of the evils or the dangers
of the policy he was pursuing. It would
hardly be possible to recruit the support of
other men in parliament save by making
reference to points of misgovernment which
one was prepared to specify. On the other
hand, such a man would be able to predict
in advance that while Walpole was minister
ample opportunities would arise for plausible criticism. Newcastle and Hardwicke
knew in advance in 1762 that Bute would
provide them with what they could claim
to be reasonable pretexts for opposition;
though when Newcastle thought that the
Treaty of Paris met the case, Hardwicke
disagreed and said that it would be better
to wait for more genuine offences which
were bound to come.[7] In certain senses it
was possible to oppose not merely the mistakes of ministers but also the alleged scandal of their actual appointment. While the
Pelhams were in power one might complain that the hand of the king had been
forced by a political combination. When a
Carteret or a Bute had the king's confi-
[7] Yorke, *Hardwicke*, III, 444.

dence, one could cry out against the evils
of favouritism and closet influence. If in
the one case the argument would be partly
sincere and partly tactical, the same would
be true in the other case too.

In this situation, it is artificial to speak of
the king's rights in a legalistic manner, or
to imagine them as existing in a vacuum.
If George III did not laudably take a calculated risk in order to free Britain from the
dangers of an oligarchical combination, he
brought much trouble upon himself and his
kingdom by taking too literally his formal
right to choose his own confidant and minister. It might even be said that he tried
to put into execution the Namier theory
of government — a theory based on isolated
and specialized considerations. And certainly he had a "right" (in a sense) to try
the experiment, provided he was ready to
face the music or to take arms against a sea
of troubles. But he was wrong if he expected the Namier theory of government
to save him from the obvious political consequences of his actions. And some of the
very people who were on his side showed
their sense of the magnitude of the risk that
was being taken. The point is, that a king
had to learn by the hard way or by the easy
way that there were certain forms of self-
assertion that were hardly going to be worth
attempting. They provoked too much
trouble, made government too inconvenient, brought out the latent conflict in the
constitution, and were calculated to limit
still further the choices that would be open
to the king next time.

This flexible view of the constitution is
by no means the invention of the modern
historian. The *Annual Register* for 1763
supported David Hume in the opinion that
the Stuarts themselves had erred not by
extending the prerogative but by failing to
see that the time had come for a loosening
of the reins. It was prepared to entertain
the idea of putting new restrictions on the
king — going further than the existing
laws actually went — though judging
against the necessity of the policy on that
immediate occasion. It described the party

of Newcastle as objecting to the appointment of Bute not because it was formally illegitimate but because it was against "the spirit of the constitution." Already there were people who were using this formula for the purpose of measuring the letter of the constitution against some notion of its deeper intent.

On this whole issue, let us be clear that, if the principle of monarchy had survived a succession of revolutions, there is no reason to believe that men had forgotten the triumph of Whiggism in the Hanoverian succession. Indeed, amongst the victors of 1688 had been a Whig interpretation of history which was itself based on a kind of constitutional doctrine — the view that liberty and the parliamentary system were coeval with the monarchy, inherent in English history, and never a mere concession from kings. Those who emphasize the quasi-technical rights of the monarch in the eighteenth century must remember also the enormous influence of Locke in what was really a wide realm of thought. It would not be easy in the eighteenth century to lose sight of the fact that in England — and even before the Revolution of 1688 — there was something of a tradition of resistance to kings. In England there was nothing to stop the beaten candidate, the would-be minister, from seeking to rouse the house of commons against his successful rival. He could do this if he was ready to brave the king's displeasure — a displeasure which (however severely the king might threaten it) would not necessarily prove eternal. And, whatever lip-service men might give to the idea that regular opposition was disloyal, Englishmen by 1760 must have become accustomed to the existence of the phenomenon.

IV

From the middle of the nineteenth century it was realized that eighteenth-century politics were not to be interpreted in terms of the Victorian two-party system. Certain breaks in continuity had been noted and it had been pointed out, for example, that the Whigs of the age of Rockingham appeared to have borrowed something from the Tory opposition of Walpole's day. It had been seen that the struggle between Whig and Tory had been complicated by another pattern of conflict — the rivalry of political clans or connections, fighting under a lord and recruited from his relatives, his clients and his political associates. All the time, of course, it had been recognized that the distinction between Whig and Tory had been prolonged for factious purposes after it had ceased to be relevant to the situation. It was realized in any case that parties in the eighteenth century differed greatly from those of more recent times, and that these varying types must not be confused or identified with one another. At the same time, Sir Lewis Namier and his followers have made a tremendous advance in our knowledge and appreciation of the non-party elements in the politics of the period, though the existence — and, to a certain degree, the importance — of these (whether independent members of the house of commons or "King's Friends") had not passed unnoticed.

But the anatomical methods of the Namier school have been producing in various periods of the eighteenth century a serious divergence on the whole subject of party between their view and that of the more comprehensive narrative historians, whether of the past or of the present. The organization of the issues of the time into a straight conflict between Whig and Tory, if it ever existed in a pure form, had been qualified in the course of time, but had still been carried to the point of exaggeration. Now, however, the divorce of the idea of Whig and Tory from what are sometimes regarded as the purely factional conflicts of the time, has tended to become too great, and a number of historians seem to have been uneasy about it. It might be claimed that the mere analysis of "the structure of politics" is not sufficient for an over-all judgment — that a knowledge of the full political story of the time is necessary for a comprehensive view of the working of the system — that, indeed, the parliamentary debates, in so far as they are recoverable, are important, as well as the division-lists. We might go further and say that all the workings and policies of government offices and departments require to be studied and elucidated before the structure of government itself (as well as the direction of government action) can be comprehensively surveyed. Perhaps we might even say that, without the full narrative, it is impossible for the student to have a complete view of "the structure of politics" itself. The Namier form of procedure certainly seems to allow those who adopt it to miss the point of certain imponderables on occasion; and at times its followers tend to overlook anything so vague and cloudy as the Whig consciousness or the Whig tradition — which is a question relating to human minds. In this way one can come to react too violently against the older Whig interpretation of history, reducing the Rockinghamite connection too much to the level of a merely factious combination, or making it too much like the other political groups of the time. Sir Lewis Namier, while rightly insisting on the importance of party in the development of limited monarchy in England, seems at times to under-estimate the effect which the earlier, less adequate, forms of political combination had in the eighteenth century, even before 1760 for example. And he does less than justice to the way in which men had long been consciously striving to achieve a more logical form of party. He does less than justice, also, to the amount of writing and theorizing which was devoted to the problem, and which, even when it purported to attack the idea of party, was really seeking a new form of it that would be more relevant to current issues. Indeed, if we accept his theory concerning the importance of party in the development of limited monarchy, we must regard George III as shrewd in respect of his monarchical interests when he repeatedly expressed his desire to destroy party, whether in the sense of Whig and Tory or in the sense of aristo-cratic political connection. And, by the same argument, the Rockinghamites were right when they protested that the destruction of these kinds of political combination would enhance the royal power.

It would not be wrong, of course, to describe the government of the earlier Hanoverians as "Whig." We must keep our sense of humour and not imagine that the Walpoles and Pelhams had ceased to be Whigs because — having secured a king who was on their side and who conformed to the will of the nation (as they saw it) — they suspended their anti-prerogative teaching, and their reserve doctrine of resistance, desiring first and foremost to make the Hanoverian succession secure. I do not believe that the Walpoles and Hardwickes, the Pelhams and Rockinghams — and that body sometimes designated as "the old corps" — ever for a moment forgot that they belonged to the great Whig tradition. Horace Walpole could support the government in the days of the early Hanoverians, and could even rejoice to see the Duke of Newcastle overthrown by George III. But the Whig tradition did mean a great deal to him, and, in 1756, he tells us how he keeps at the side of his bed not only *Magna Carta* but also the warrant for Charles I's execution. And this we can take as something more than an infatuation over dead issues and battles long ago. Though the Tories were not likely to bring out prerogative doctrines for the benefit of Hanoverian kings who were in the pockets of the Whigs, their tradition persisted, perhaps anomalously, in the localities. It seems to have endured in the form of high church prejudice after the religious issue had ceased to be important in parliamentary politics.

Even after 1760 the *Annual Register* showed how the Duke of Newcastle had come to be the head of a body which it simply designated as "the Whigs." When the Marquess of Rockingham had succeeded him in the leadership, his papers still described the connection as "the Whigs," *tout court*. Horace Walpole, in his *Memoirs of the Reign of George III,* repeatedly uses the term "the Whigs" when it is clear that he is referring to the Rockinghamites. Even if this party had arrogated the title to themselves unfairly, the fact would confirm the view that some association with the Whig tradition was either in their desire or in their consciousness. But when the Duke of Cumberland was negotiating for the establishment of the ministry of 1765, he too spoke of treating not only with Temple and Pitt but also "with those lords that formed the head of the Whig party." Newcastle played his part in that negotiation, and meetings were held at his house, though when the arrangement finally took form it was Rockingham who was charged with the conduct of the new administration. Newcastle still retained his connection with the party, however — grumbling when his advice was sometimes ignored — and it would be wrong to suggest that Rockingham now emerged as the new leader of a new party. Some derision has been poured on the idea that the Rockinghamites were *"sui generis* among eighteenth-century parties;" but, if all consciousness of intellectual tradition were drained out of the story, the truth remains that such bodies as the "Bedford Whigs" were rather like clans and in any case were comparatively diminutive affairs. The party of Newcastle and Rockingham was even structurally different — a confederacy between clans, or between the heads of clans — still conscious, even in 1792, of standing as the representative of the aristocratic interest of the country — but less like a clan and more like a "party" when a Walpole, instead of a powerful magnate, could have the political leadership of the whole confederacy.

It is possible that the ubiquity of party in the present-day house of commons, the hardness of party organization and the firmness of party discipline have begun to affect the attitude of the historian to eighteenth century parliamentary life. Even within the twentieth century there have been many people who started their thinking on

this subject from a different norm, and had misgivings about the growing severity of party discipline, the reduction of freedom and independence, the decline in the rôle of the private member, and the little effect that the course of debate seemed to have on divisions. In 1767 Rockingham's papers show his party as numbering 121, while the Duke of Newcastle put the figure at 101. These two men provide us with lists which, since they were meant for internal use, can hardly have been intended to deceive; yet they diverge from one another, having 77 names in common, but enumerating a considerable body of men whose attachment must have been doubtful or occasional. It is easy for the historian to say: "What kind of party was it whose leaders did not know their own followers?" But we must expect just such signs of more primitive structure when we are dealing with an earlier period of history. In fact, it has long been realized that the political connections of the eighteenth century did not possess the solidarity of modern party-organization, and that parliamentary life was less regimented than now. It is only too likely that parties inside parliament in that period — perhaps like parties outside parliament today — would have a broad vague fringe, with some people attached to one leader rather than another, or associated for one type of purpose but not for all. Over a decade after 1767, the band of men around Charles James Fox seemed to be skirmishing only in somewhat loose alliance with the Marquess of Rockingham. We are told that on 17 February 1768, only between 50 and 60 of the men who had been claimed for the party voted for the *Nullum Tempus* Bill, to which Rockingham attached great importance. But if we must not expect the tightness of modern party organization, we must not expect the modern tightness of party discipline in the eighteenth century. Men who "had close ties with the magnates of the Rockingham party" would certainly fail to follow their chief on occasion; it was notoriously difficult to secure attendance in parliament, and important people might refuse to resist the lure of Newmarket. When we are told that a party leader could not absolutely "count on the votes of his closest followers" we show how much we have forgotten if we allow ourselves to be too surprised. Furthermore, it is not this — it is the rigidity of modern party discipline that presents the paradox and requires to be explained. The fact that party was so loose a combination — so vague at the edges and so fluid internally — is surely one of the reasons why we must be careful about making hard inferences from statistics and division lists. Two separate accounts (Horace Walpole and the *Parliamentary History*) suggest that, in the case of the *Nullum Tempus* Bill, the actual course of the debate has some relevance in a discussion of the division-lists. And the fact that in 1767 Rockingham could say, while negotiating on behalf of his party, "that he was responsible to a large body of people for his conduct" may be more significant of the relative standing of his party than the actual figures we possess. We need not accept his words with superstitious credulity; but he was speaking to Grafton who would surely have recognized anything that was obviously foolish. Mr. Brooke, who provides us with these figures and discusses the whole issue in his book on *The Chatham Administration,* has greatly added to our knowledge by his researches and has produced a work that is indispensable to students of this period. But, until further evidence is provided, the outside student might question some of his inferences from the evidence and may doubt whether, on the subject of the Rockinghamites, he has not carried the reaction against the Whig interpretation too far.

The Duke of Newcastle was not dismissed in 1762; he resigned because he would no longer accept the terms on which he was expected to collaborate with his colleague, Bute. It is sometimes objected that he and Rockingham opposed the King and the government merely because they were out of office; but one can answer that these men and their friends might easily have had office if they had been prepared to accept it at any price. At least we must say that there was some article (or some form) of independence which they felt that they were called upon to sacrifice if they worked with the new régime. On this issue, to be sure, we can wipe them out as merely arrogant or selfish if we have decided beforehand that we will be on the side of the King. Even when Bute was out of office the supporters of Newcastle still directed their hostility against the Favourite's influence (or his possible influence) in the Closet. Later, when the Rockingham ministry was falling in 1766, both its friends and its enemies imputed its weakness to the intransigeance which it showed towards Bute's party, the men who were later known as the King's Friends. At the next stage in the story, the dismissal of Rockingham was exactly calculated to raise the issue of Closet intrigues carried on behind the backs of the ministry of the day. Clearly the political developments of the time had brought to an intenser stage the problem that had existed under the earlier Hanoverians — whether in the case of Hanoverian advisers or the case of Carteret in 1746 — the question of the confidence which was due from the King to the ministers who were conducting his affairs in parliament. The successive examples of opposition to Bute help us to see why Horace Walpole regarded the party of Newcastle and Rockingham as showing a greater consistency than other parties. The Rockinghamites elaborated their ideas as they opposed the claims of the court in regard to both the appointment and the treatment of ministers. In one form or another they raised the crucial question of the relations between the Closet and the Ministry, a question particularly congenial to men who felt themselves to be in the Whig tradition. It is remarkable to see how early these men had begun to adumbrate — though in a context so unlike our later one — the features of our modern constitution, at least in respect of the position of ministers. In his *Thoughts on the Causes of the Present Discontents,* Edmund Burke, in 1770, went to the heart of this particular issue. He conceded that George III might not have broken any laws in this connection, but, using the formula which we have already met at the beginning of the reign, he insisted that the choice of ministers on any but public grounds was against "the spirit of the constitution." He also took his stand on the principle of "party" as such, and made this in itself a further issue with the monarchy; and it is difficult to see why Sir Lewis Namier, who sees the importance of "party" in the establishment of an effectively limited monarchy, should be so anxious to deny the contribution of the Rockinghamites to this whole process of development. However technically "correct" George III may have been in respect to the ministerial problem, surely it will not be argued that it would have been better to leave him without serious opposition — as though it were a misfortune that there existed a body of men who had an alternative view of the direction in which they desired to see the constitution develop.

Horace Walpole takes the line that the two main parties of Whig and Tory went on existing for a few years after George III's accession to the throne. Even in the ensuing confusion of parties, however, he makes a clear dividing-line, and it is interesting to see that he has a guiding principle. He shows that he will regard as "Tories" the men who support the prerogative or have a leaning towards arbitrary government. He will call them "Tories" even if they go on calling themselves "Whigs," and even if, like Lord North they really are Whigs in the more superficial and conventional sense — supporters of the Revolution and the Hanoverian settlement.[8] But,

he adds, the men who were on the side of the court, though they never actually disclaimed the title of "Whig," ceased to call themselves by that term. For Horace Walpole, then, the issues were beginning to sort themselves out again, and a situation was being produced in which political "connection" might be more reasonably related to political "principle." The situation was not as logical as this might suggest, and even in the days of Gilbert and Sullivan the old idea of party based on "connection" was still anomalously entangled with the idea of party based on principle — for why otherwise should we have had the song about being "born" a little liberal or a little conservative? And it is not irrelevant to note that, according to Walpole, the Opposition dates back to the resistance that was offered to Bute.

Whether we are dealing with the king's right to choose his ministers, or the state of the constitution (and of contemporary opinions about the constitution) or the supposed inadmissibility of regular opposition, or the alleged non-existence of party, other than selfish faction, it is necessary that we should not allow any inflexibility of mind, any literalness of interpretation, to take away the importance of the problems provoked by the régime of Bute, or to argue that the constitutional issue was illegitimate, or — even if it was illegitimate — to pretend that it did not exist in the controversies of the time. It is not clear that the historical method which has been described as "counting the cabbage-patches in Ohio"

---

[8] Sir Lewis Namier, in *Personalities and Powers,* p. 33, asserts that Horace Walpole, when he called North a "Tory" (in a footnote added in the 1780's), was merely resorting to "current cant." One would like to see him write more fully upon the whole passage to which this footnote is appended; for Walpole had been describing

how, though few real Tories had been admitted into place, a number of people who called themselves Whigs had gone over to Bute's prerogative doctrines. Under Lord North, he says, "the Court's system of prerogative predominated entirely." It is not clear that Sir Lewis Namier, in his talk of "current cant," is not under-estimating the genuineness of the Whig tradition in Walpole and the possible authenticity of a certain "Whiggish" attitude to the régime of North. Also he omits the fact that Walpole had just declared the system of Whig party versus Tory party to have dissolved, so that there was room for the new division which he was trying to make on a point of principle. [See H. Walpole, *Memoirs of the Reign of King George III* (1894), Vol. II, p. 66.]

(though it has much utility in its own more obvious sphere) has not — by a certain literalism and unimaginativeness — carried us further from the truth. It neglects the importance of constituencies like those of the metropolitan area, where public opinion had its place in political life; underrates the significance of appeals to extra-parliamentary opinion, such as are seen even in the age of *The Craftsman*; shows too little regard for the attempts which were made even before 1760 to measure the house of commons against at least the presumed rights and opinions of constituents; and fails to trace the whole story of the development of political consciousness in the nation at large. Like the Whig tradition, these things are sieved away, as "imponderables" by the Namier technique, and with them disappears that whole aspect of politics which addresses itself to public opinion, and which certainly the *Annual Register* would hardly have recorded if it had not been there.

SUGGESTIONS FOR ADDITIONAL READING

The suggestions in this reading list do not attempt to cover all aspects of the reign, but only those works which relate to the political questions of the early part of the reign. The best general introduction to the period is J. Steven Watson, *The Reign of George III, 1760–1815* (Oxford, 1960) in the *Oxford History of England* series. This volume, like the others in the series, concentrates on political history but gives attention to other aspects of the period. It includes an up-to-date bibliography. *The Dictionary of National Biography* (London, 1917) is especially strong on the eighteenth century. Although the articles are now dated, they were written by the best authorities of the time and the authors were given sufficient space to make their articles useful to the specialist as well as to the general reader. The modern approach to the politics of the reign of George III begins with the two major works of Sir Lewis Namier, *The Structure of Politics at the Accession of George III* (2nd ed., London, 1957) and *England in the Age of the American Revolution* (2nd ed., London, 1961). The best general analysis of the operation of politics is Richard Pares, *King George III and the Politicians* (Oxford, 1953). Two volumes in a new series entitled *English Historical Documents* supply extensive documents and excellent introductions and bibliographies. These are volume X (1714–83), edited by D. B. Horn and Mary Ransome (New York, 1957) and volume XI (1783–1832), edited by A. Aspinall and E. Anthony Smith (New York, 1959). A convenient one-volume collection of documents is E. Neville Williams, *The Eighteenth Century Constitution, 1688–1815* (Cambridge, 1960).

Much of the correspondence of political leaders has been published, although some editions leave much to be desired. For George III see *The Correspondence of King George the Third from 1760 to December, 1783*, ed. by Sir John Fortescue, 6 vols. (London, 1927–28). The many errors in this edition are pointed out in Sir Lewis Namier's *Additions and Corrections to Sir John Fortescue's Edition* (Manchester, 1938). Unfortunately, Fortescue's edition was good enough so that it has not seemed worth doing again, and not good enough to be used with complete confidence. Romney Sedgwick's *Letters from George III to Lord Bute, 1756–1766* (London, 1939) is an editorial masterpiece. For the latter part of the reign a fine modern edition of George III's papers and correspondence is being published under the editorship of A. Aspinall. Two volumes of *The Later Correspondence of George III* (Cambridge, 1962, 1963) have already appeared.

The middle of the nineteenth century

saw the publication of the works and correspondence of many of the political leaders of the eighteenth century. These collections of source material and the introductions of the editors were important in shaping the interpretation of the reign of George III. Among the most important of these were the *Correspondence of William Pitt, Earl of Chatham,* ed. by W. S. Taylor and J. H. Pringle, 4 vols. (London, 1838–40); the *Correspondence of John, Fourth Duke of Bedford,* ed. by Lord John Russell, 3 vols. (London, 1842); *The Works and Correspondence of the Right Honourable Edmund Burke,* 8 vols. (London, 1852); *Memorials and Correspondence of Charles James Fox,* ed. by Lord John Russell, 4 vols. (London, 1853–57); *The Grenville Papers,* ed. by W. J. Smith, 4 vols. (London, 1852–53); *Memoirs of the Marquis of Rockingham,* ed. by George T. K. Albemarle (London, 1852); *The Journal and Correspondence of William [Eden], Lord Auckland,* 4 vols. (London, 1861–62); Lord Edmond Fitzmaurice, *Life of William, Earl of Shelburne,* 3 vols. (London, 1875–76); and the *Autobiography of the Duke of Grafton* (London, 1898). Some modern collections of source materials which are of great value are *The Parliamentary Papers of John Robinson,* ed. by W. T. Laprade (London, 1922); the *Jenkinson Papers,* ed. by Ninetta Jucker (London, 1949); and the new editions of the correspondence of Horace Walpole, ed. by W. S. Lewis, published by the Yale University Press and Edmund Burke, with Thomas W. Copeland the general editor, published by the University of Chicago Press. At some time in his life every scholar of the reign of George III, and the sooner the better, has worked his way through these collections of documents.

From the great mass of specialized literature on the reign of George III the following works have been chosen as being of special importance or unusual interest to students: Colwyn C. Vulliamy, *Royal George: A Study of King George III* (New York, 1937); Roger Fulford, *Royal Dukes* (London, 1933); Raymond Postgate, *That Devil Wilkes* (New York, 1929); Charles Chenevix Trench, *Portrait of a Patriot: A Biography of John Wilkes* (London, 1962); S. Maccoby, *English Radicalism, 1762–1785* (London, 1955); George Rudé, *Wilkes and Liberty* (Oxford, 1962); John Brooke, *The Chatham Administration* (New York, 1956); Ian Christie, *The End of North's Ministry* (London, 1958) and *Wilkes, Wyvill and Reform* (London, 1962); Herbert Butterfield, *George III, Lord North, and the People, 1779–1780* (London, 1949); Donald Barnes, *George III and William Pitt, 1783–1806* (Stanford, 1939); Carl Cone, *Burke and the Nature of Politics* (Lexington, Ky., 1957); Lucy Sutherland, "The City of London in Eighteenth-Century Politics," in *Essays Presented to Sir Lewis Namier,* ed. by Richard Pares and A. J. P. Taylor (London, 1956); David Lindsay Keir, "Economical Reform, 1779–1787," *Law Quarterly Review* (July, 1934); A. S. Foord, "The Waning of the 'Influence of the Crown'," *English Historical Review* (LXII, 1947).